Dear Future Exam Success Story

First of all, **THANK YOU** for purchasing Mometrix study materials!

Second, congratulations! You are one of the few determined test-takers who are committed to doing whatever it takes to excel on your exam. **You have come to the right place.** We developed these study materials with one goal in mind: to deliver you the information you need in a format that's concise and easy to use.

In addition to optimizing your guide for the content of the test, we've outlined our recommended steps for breaking down the preparation process into small, attainable goals so you can make sure you stay on track.

We've also analyzed the entire test-taking process, identifying the most common pitfalls and showing how you can overcome them and be ready for any curveball the test throws you.

Standardized testing is one of the biggest obstacles on your road to success, which only increases the importance of doing well in the high-pressure, high-stakes environment of test day. Your results on this test could have a significant impact on your future, and this guide provides the information and practical advice to help you achieve your full potential on test day.

Your success is our success

We would love to hear from you! If you would like to share the story of your exam success or if you have any questions or comments in regard to our products, please contact us at **800-673-8175** or **support@mometrix.com**.

Thanks again for your business and we wish you continued success!

Sincerely,
The Mometrix Test Preparation Team

Need more help? Check out our flashcards at:
http://MometrixFlashcards.com/GACE

I0893673

Written and edited by the Mometrix Exam Secrets Test Prep Team
Printed in the United States of America

Mometrix
TEST PREPARATION

GACE

Political Science Secrets Study Guide

TABLE OF CONTENTS

Introduction

Thank you for purchasing this resource! You have made the choice to prepare yourself for a test that could have a huge impact on your future, and this guide is designed to help you be fully ready for test day. Obviously, it's important to have a solid understanding of the test material, but you also need to be prepared for the unique environment and stressors of the test, so that you can perform to the best of your abilities.

For this purpose, the first section that appears in this guide is the **Secret Keys**. We've devoted countless hours to meticulously researching what works and what doesn't, and we've boiled down our findings to the five most impactful steps you can take to improve your performance on the test. We start at the beginning with study planning and move through the preparation process, all the way to the testing strategies that will help you get the most out of what you know when you're finally sitting in front of the test.

We recommend that you start preparing for your test as far in advance as possible. However, if you've bought this guide as a last-minute study resource and only have a few days before your test, we recommend that you skip over the first two Secret Keys since they address a long-term study plan.

If you struggle with **test anxiety**, we strongly encourage you to check out our recommendations for how you can overcome it. Test anxiety is a formidable foe, but it can be beaten, and we want to make sure you have the tools you need to defeat it.

Secret Key #1 – Plan Big, Study Small

There's a lot riding on your performance. If you want to ace this test, you're going to need to keep your skills sharp and the material fresh in your mind. You need a plan that lets you review everything you need to know while still fitting in your schedule. We'll break this strategy down into three categories.

Information Organization

Start with the information you already have: the official test outline. From this, you can make a complete list of all the concepts you need to cover before the test. Organize these concepts into groups that can be studied together, and create a list of any related vocabulary you need to learn so you can brush up on any difficult terms. You'll want to keep this vocabulary list handy once you actually start studying since you may need to add to it along the way.

Time Management

Once you have your set of study concepts, decide how to spread them out over the time you have left before the test. Break your study plan into small, clear goals so you have a manageable task for each day and know exactly what you're doing. Then just focus on one small step at a time. When you manage your time this way, you don't need to spend hours at a time studying. Studying a small block of content for a short period each day helps you retain information better and avoid stressing over how much you have left to do. You can relax knowing that you have a plan to cover everything in time. In order for this strategy to be effective though, you have to start studying early and stick to your schedule. Avoid the exhaustion and futility that comes from last-minute cramming!

Study Environment

The environment you study in has a big impact on your learning. Studying in a coffee shop, while probably more enjoyable, is not likely to be as fruitful as studying in a quiet room. It's important to keep distractions to a minimum. You're only planning to study for a short block of time, so make the most of it. Don't pause to check your phone or get up to find a snack. It's also important to **avoid multitasking**. Research has consistently shown that multitasking will make your studying dramatically less effective. Your study area should also be comfortable and well-lit so you don't have the distraction of straining your eyes or sitting on an uncomfortable chair.

The time of day you study is also important. You want to be rested and alert. Don't wait until just before bedtime. Study when you'll be most likely to comprehend and remember. Even better, if you know what time of day your test will be, set that time aside for study. That way your brain will be used to working on that subject at that specific time and you'll have a better chance of recalling information.

Finally, it can be helpful to team up with others who are studying for the same test. Your actual studying should be done in as isolated an environment as possible, but the work of organizing the information and setting up the study plan can be divided up. In between study sessions, you can discuss with your teammates the concepts that you're all studying and quiz each other on the details. Just be sure that your teammates are as serious about the test as you are. If you find that your study time is being replaced with social time, you might need to find a new team.

Secret Key #2 – Make Your Studying Count

You're devoting a lot of time and effort to preparing for this test, so you want to be absolutely certain it will pay off. This means doing more than just reading the content and hoping you can remember it on test day. It's important to make every minute of study count. There are two main areas you can focus on to make your studying count.

Retention

It doesn't matter how much time you study if you can't remember the material. You need to make sure you are retaining the concepts. To check your retention of the information you're learning, try recalling it at later times with minimal prompting. Try carrying around flashcards and glance at one or two from time to time or ask a friend who's also studying for the test to quiz you.

To enhance your retention, look for ways to put the information into practice so that you can apply it rather than simply recalling it. If you're using the information in practical ways, it will be much easier to remember. Similarly, it helps to solidify a concept in your mind if you're not only reading it to yourself but also explaining it to someone else. Ask a friend to let you teach them about a concept you're a little shaky on (or speak aloud to an imaginary audience if necessary). As you try to summarize, define, give examples, and answer your friend's questions, you'll understand the concepts better and they will stay with you longer. Finally, step back for a big picture view and ask yourself how each piece of information fits with the whole subject. When you link the different concepts together and see them working together as a whole, it's easier to remember the individual components.

Finally, practice showing your work on any multi-step problems, even if you're just studying. Writing out each step you take to solve a problem will help solidify the process in your mind, and you'll be more likely to remember it during the test.

Modality

Modality simply refers to the means or method by which you study. Choosing a study modality that fits your own individual learning style is crucial. No two people learn best in exactly the same way, so it's important to know your strengths and use them to your advantage.

For example, if you learn best by visualization, focus on visualizing a concept in your mind and draw an image or a diagram. Try color-coding your notes, illustrating them, or creating symbols that will trigger your mind to recall a learned concept. If you learn best by hearing or discussing information, find a study partner who learns the same way or read aloud to yourself. Think about how to put the information in your own words. Imagine that you are giving a lecture on the topic and record yourself so you can listen to it later.

For any learning style, flashcards can be helpful. Organize the information so you can take advantage of spare moments to review. Underline key words or phrases. Use different colors for different categories. Mnemonic devices (such as creating a short list in which every item starts with the same letter) can also help with retention. Find what works best for you and use it to store the information in your mind most effectively and easily.

Secret Key #3 – Practice the Right Way

Your success on test day depends not only on how many hours you put into preparing, but also on whether you prepared the right way. It's good to check along the way to see if your studying is paying off. One of the most effective ways to do this is by taking practice tests to evaluate your progress. Practice tests are useful because they show exactly where you need to improve. Every time you take a practice test, pay special attention to these three groups of questions:

- The questions you got wrong
- The questions you had to guess on, even if you guessed right
- The questions you found difficult or slow to work through

This will show you exactly what your weak areas are, and where you need to devote more study time. Ask yourself why each of these questions gave you trouble. Was it because you didn't understand the material? Was it because you didn't remember the vocabulary? Do you need more repetitions on this type of question to build speed and confidence? Dig into those questions and figure out how you can strengthen your weak areas as you go back to review the material.

Additionally, many practice tests have a section explaining the answer choices. It can be tempting to read the explanation and think that you now have a good understanding of the concept. However, an explanation likely only covers part of the question's broader context. Even if the explanation makes perfect sense, **go back and investigate** every concept related to the question until you're positive you have a thorough understanding.

As you go along, keep in mind that the practice test is just that: practice. Memorizing these questions and answers will not be very helpful on the actual test because it is unlikely to have any of the same exact questions. If you only know the right answers to the sample questions, you won't be prepared for the real thing. **Study the concepts** until you understand them fully, and then you'll be able to answer any question that shows up on the test.

It's important to wait on the practice tests until you're ready. If you take a test on your first day of study, you may be overwhelmed by the amount of material covered and how much you need to learn. Work up to it gradually.

On test day, you'll need to be prepared for answering questions, managing your time, and using the test-taking strategies you've learned. It's a lot to balance, like a mental marathon that will have a big impact on your future. Like training for a marathon, you'll need to start slowly and work your way up. When test day arrives, you'll be ready.

Start with the strategies you've read in the first two Secret Keys—plan your course and study in the way that works best for you. If you have time, consider using multiple study resources to get different approaches to the same concepts. It can be helpful to see difficult concepts from more than one angle. Then find a good source for practice tests. Many times, the test website will suggest potential study resources or provide sample tests.

Practice Test Strategy

If you're able to find at least three practice tests, we recommend this strategy:

Untimed and Open-Book Practice

Take the first test with no time constraints and with your notes and study guide handy. Take your time and focus on applying the strategies you've learned.

Timed and Open-Book Practice

Take the second practice test open-book as well, but set a timer and practice pacing yourself to finish in time.

Timed and Closed-Book Practice

Take any other practice tests as if it were test day. Set a timer and put away your study materials. Sit at a table or desk in a quiet room, imagine yourself at the testing center, and answer questions as quickly and accurately as possible.

Keep repeating timed and closed-book tests on a regular basis until you run out of practice tests or it's time for the actual test. Your mind will be ready for the schedule and stress of test day, and you'll be able to focus on recalling the material you've learned.

Secret Key #4 – Pace Yourself

Once you're fully prepared for the material on the test, your biggest challenge on test day will be managing your time. Just knowing that the clock is ticking can make you panic even if you have plenty of time left. Work on pacing yourself so you can build confidence against the time constraints of the exam. Pacing is a difficult skill to master, especially in a high-pressure environment, so **practice is vital**.

Set time expectations for your pace based on how much time is available. For example, if a section has 60 questions and the time limit is 30 minutes, you know you have to average 30 seconds or less per question in order to answer them all. Although 30 seconds is the hard limit, set 25 seconds per question as your goal, so you reserve extra time to spend on harder questions. When you budget extra time for the harder questions, you no longer have any reason to stress when those questions take longer to answer.

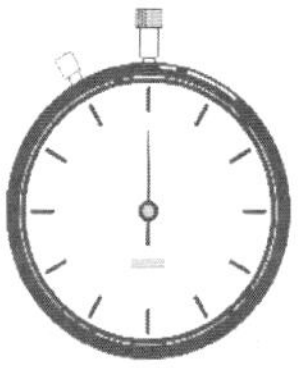

Don't let this time expectation distract you from working through the test at a calm, steady pace, but keep it in mind so you don't spend too much time on any one question. Recognize that taking extra time on one question you don't understand may keep you from answering two that you do understand later in the test. If your time limit for a question is up and you're still not sure of the answer, mark it and move on, and come back to it later if the time and the test format allow. If the testing format doesn't allow you to return to earlier questions, just make an educated guess; then put it out of your mind and move on.

On the easier questions, be careful not to rush. It may seem wise to hurry through them so you have more time for the challenging ones, but it's not worth missing one if you know the concept and just didn't take the time to read the question fully. Work efficiently but make sure you understand the question and have looked at all of the answer choices, since more than one may seem right at first.

Even if you're paying attention to the time, you may find yourself a little behind at some point. You should speed up to get back on track, but do so wisely. Don't panic; just take a few seconds less on each question until you're caught up. Don't guess without thinking, but do look through the answer choices and eliminate any you know are wrong. If you can get down to two choices, it is often worthwhile to guess from those. Once you've chosen an answer, move on and don't dwell on any that you skipped or had to hurry through. If a question was taking too long, chances are it was one of the harder ones, so you weren't as likely to get it right anyway.

On the other hand, if you find yourself getting ahead of schedule, it may be beneficial to slow down a little. The more quickly you work, the more likely you are to make a careless mistake that will affect your score. You've budgeted time for each question, so don't be afraid to spend that time. Practice an efficient but careful pace to get the most out of the time you have.

Secret Key #5 – Have a Plan for Guessing

When you're taking the test, you may find yourself stuck on a question. Some of the answer choices seem better than others, but you don't see the one answer choice that is obviously correct. What do you do?

The scenario described above is very common, yet most test takers have not effectively prepared for it. Developing and practicing a plan for guessing may be one of the single most effective uses of your time as you get ready for the exam.

In developing your plan for guessing, there are three questions to address:

- When should you start the guessing process?
- How should you narrow down the choices?
- Which answer should you choose?

When to Start the Guessing Process

Unless your plan for guessing is to select C every time (which, despite its merits, is not what we recommend), you need to leave yourself enough time to apply your answer elimination strategies. Since you have a limited amount of time for each question, that means that if you're going to give yourself the best shot at guessing correctly, you have to decide quickly whether or not you will guess.

Of course, the best-case scenario is that you don't have to guess at all, so first, see if you can answer the question based on your knowledge of the subject and basic reasoning skills. Focus on the key words in the question and try to jog your memory of related topics. Give yourself a chance to bring the knowledge to mind, but once you realize that you don't have (or you can't access) the knowledge you need to answer the question, it's time to start the guessing process.

It's almost always better to start the guessing process too early than too late. It only takes a few seconds to remember something and answer the question from knowledge. Carefully eliminating wrong answer choices takes longer. Plus, going through the process of eliminating answer choices can actually help jog your memory.

Summary: Start the guessing process as soon as you decide that you can't answer the question based on your knowledge.

How to Narrow Down the Choices

The next chapter in this book (**Test-Taking Strategies**) includes a wide range of strategies for how to approach questions and how to look for answer choices to eliminate. You will definitely want to read those carefully, practice them, and figure out which ones work best for you. Here though, we're going to address a mindset rather than a particular strategy.

Your odds of guessing an answer correctly depend on how many options you are choosing from.

Number of options left	5	4	3	2	1
Odds of guessing correctly	20%	25%	33%	50%	100%

You can see from this chart just how valuable it is to be able to eliminate incorrect answers and make an educated guess, but there are two things that many test takers do that cause them to miss out on the benefits of guessing:

- Accidentally eliminating the correct answer
- Selecting an answer based on an impression

We'll look at the first one here, and the second one in the next section.

To avoid accidentally eliminating the correct answer, we recommend a thought exercise called **the $5 challenge**. In this challenge, you only eliminate an answer choice from contention if you are willing to bet $5 on it being wrong. Why $5? Five dollars is a small but not insignificant amount of money. It's an amount you could afford to lose but wouldn't want to throw away. And while losing $5 once might not hurt too much, doing it twenty times will set you back $100. In the same way, each small decision you make—eliminating a choice here, guessing on a question there—won't by itself impact your score very much, but when you put them all together, they can make a big difference. By holding each answer choice elimination decision to a higher standard, you can reduce the risk of accidentally eliminating the correct answer.

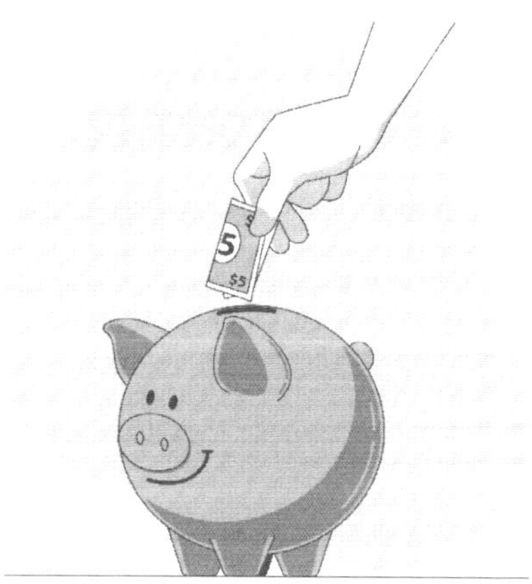

The $5 challenge can also be applied in a positive sense: If you are willing to bet $5 that an answer choice *is* correct, go ahead and mark it as correct.

Summary: Only eliminate an answer choice if you are willing to bet $5 that it is wrong.

Which Answer to Choose

You're taking the test. You've run into a hard question and decided you'll have to guess. You've eliminated all the answer choices you're willing to bet $5 on. Now you have to pick an answer. Why do we even need to talk about this? Why can't you just pick whichever one you feel like when the time comes?

The answer to these questions is that if you don't come into the test with a plan, you'll rely on your impression to select an answer choice, and if you do that, you risk falling into a trap. The test writers know that everyone who takes their test will be guessing on some of the questions, so they intentionally write wrong answer choices to seem plausible. You still have to pick an answer though, and if the wrong answer choices are designed to look right, how can you ever be sure that you're not falling for their trap? The best solution we've found to this dilemma is to take the decision out of your hands entirely. Here is the process we recommend:

Once you've eliminated any choices that you are confident (willing to bet $5) are wrong, select the first remaining choice as your answer.

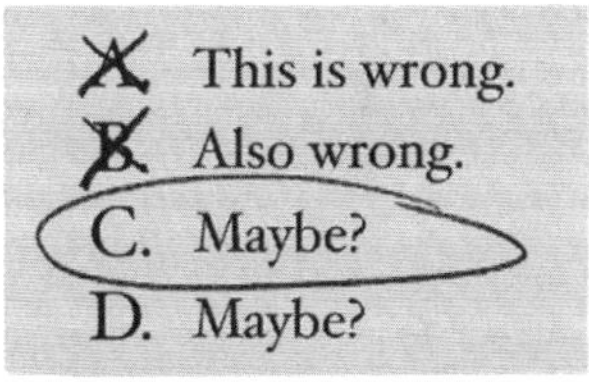

Whether you choose to select the first remaining choice, the second, or the last, the important thing is that you use some preselected standard. Using this approach guarantees that you will not be enticed into selecting an answer choice that looks right, because you are not basing your decision on how the answer choices look.

This is not meant to make you question your knowledge. Instead, it is to help you recognize the difference between your knowledge and your impressions. There's a huge difference between thinking an answer is right because of what you know, and thinking an answer is right because it looks or sounds like it should be right.

Summary: To ensure that your selection is appropriately random, make a predetermined selection from among all answer choices you have not eliminated.

Test-Taking Strategies

This section contains a list of test-taking strategies that you may find helpful as you work through the test. By taking what you know and applying logical thought, you can maximize your chances of answering any question correctly!

It is very important to realize that every question is different and every person is different: no single strategy will work on every question, and no single strategy will work for every person. That's why we've included all of them here, so you can try them out and determine which ones work best for different types of questions and which ones work best for you.

Question Strategies

✓ Read Carefully

Read the question and the answer choices carefully. Don't miss the question because you misread the terms. You have plenty of time to read each question thoroughly and make sure you understand what is being asked. Yet a happy medium must be attained, so don't waste too much time. You must read carefully and efficiently.

✓ Contextual Clues

Look for contextual clues. If the question includes a word you are not familiar with, look at the immediate context for some indication of what the word might mean. Contextual clues can often give you all the information you need to decipher the meaning of an unfamiliar word. Even if you can't determine the meaning, you may be able to narrow down the possibilities enough to make a solid guess at the answer to the question.

✓ Prefixes

If you're having trouble with a word in the question or answer choices, try dissecting it. Take advantage of every clue that the word might include. Prefixes can be a huge help. Usually, they allow you to determine a basic meaning. *Pre-* means before, *post-* means after, *pro-* is positive, *de-* is negative. From prefixes, you can get an idea of the general meaning of the word and try to put it into context.

✓ Hedge Words

Watch out for critical hedge words, such as *likely, may, can, often, almost, mostly, usually, generally, rarely,* and *sometimes.* Question writers insert these hedge phrases to cover every possibility. Often an answer choice will be wrong simply because it leaves no room for exception. Be on guard for answer choices that have definitive words such as *exactly* and *always.*

✓ Switchback Words

Stay alert for *switchbacks.* These are the words and phrases frequently used to alert you to shifts in thought. The most common switchback words are *but, although,* and *however.* Others include *nevertheless, on the other hand, even though, while, in spite of, despite,* and *regardless of.* Switchback words are important to catch because they can change the direction of the question or an answer choice.

⊘ Face Value

When in doubt, use common sense. Accept the situation in the problem at face value. Don't read too much into it. These problems will not require you to make wild assumptions. If you have to go beyond creativity and warp time or space in order to have an answer choice fit the question, then you should move on and consider the other answer choices. These are normal problems rooted in reality. The applicable relationship or explanation may not be readily apparent, but it is there for you to figure out. Use your common sense to interpret anything that isn't clear.

Answer Choice Strategies

⊘ Answer Selection

The most thorough way to pick an answer choice is to identify and eliminate wrong answers until only one is left, then confirm it is the correct answer. Sometimes an answer choice may immediately seem right, but be careful. The test writers will usually put more than one reasonable answer choice on each question, so take a second to read all of them and make sure that the other choices are not equally obvious. As long as you have time left, it is better to read every answer choice than to pick the first one that looks right without checking the others.

⊘ Answer Choice Families

An answer choice family consists of two (in rare cases, three) answer choices that are very similar in construction and cannot all be true at the same time. If you see two answer choices that are direct opposites or parallels, one of them is usually the correct answer. For instance, if one answer choice says that quantity *x* increases and another either says that quantity *x* decreases (opposite) or says that quantity *y* increases (parallel), then those answer choices would fall into the same family. An answer choice that doesn't match the construction of the answer choice family is more likely to be incorrect. Most questions will not have answer choice families, but when they do appear, you should be prepared to recognize them.

⊘ Eliminate Answers

Eliminate answer choices as soon as you realize they are wrong, but make sure you consider all possibilities. If you are eliminating answer choices and realize that the last one you are left with is also wrong, don't panic. Start over and consider each choice again. There may be something you missed the first time that you will realize on the second pass.

⊘ Avoid Fact Traps

Don't be distracted by an answer choice that is factually true but doesn't answer the question. You are looking for the choice that answers the question. Stay focused on what the question is asking for so you don't accidentally pick an answer that is true but incorrect. Always go back to the question and make sure the answer choice you've selected actually answers the question and is not merely a true statement.

⊘ Extreme Statements

In general, you should avoid answers that put forth extreme actions as standard practice or proclaim controversial ideas as established fact. An answer choice that states the "process should be used in certain situations, if…" is much more likely to be correct than one that states the "process should be discontinued completely." The first is a calm rational statement and doesn't even make a definitive, uncompromising stance, using a hedge word *if* to provide wiggle room, whereas the second choice is far more extreme.

⊘ BENCHMARK

As you read through the answer choices and you come across one that seems to answer the question well, mentally select that answer choice. This is not your final answer, but it's the one that will help you evaluate the other answer choices. The one that you selected is your benchmark or standard for judging each of the other answer choices. Every other answer choice must be compared to your benchmark. That choice is correct until proven otherwise by another answer choice beating it. If you find a better answer, then that one becomes your new benchmark. Once you've decided that no other choice answers the question as well as your benchmark, you have your final answer.

⊘ PREDICT THE ANSWER

Before you even start looking at the answer choices, it is often best to try to predict the answer. When you come up with the answer on your own, it is easier to avoid distractions and traps because you will know exactly what to look for. The right answer choice is unlikely to be word-for-word what you came up with, but it should be a close match. Even if you are confident that you have the right answer, you should still take the time to read each option before moving on.

General Strategies

⊘ TOUGH QUESTIONS

If you are stumped on a problem or it appears too hard or too difficult, don't waste time. Move on! Remember though, if you can quickly check for obviously incorrect answer choices, your chances of guessing correctly are greatly improved. Before you completely give up, at least try to knock out a couple of possible answers. Eliminate what you can and then guess at the remaining answer choices before moving on.

⊘ CHECK YOUR WORK

Since you will probably not know every term listed and the answer to every question, it is important that you get credit for the ones that you do know. Don't miss any questions through careless mistakes. If at all possible, try to take a second to look back over your answer selection and make sure you've selected the correct answer choice and haven't made a costly careless mistake (such as marking an answer choice that you didn't mean to mark). This quick double check should more than pay for itself in caught mistakes for the time it costs.

⊘ PACE YOURSELF

It's easy to be overwhelmed when you're looking at a page full of questions; your mind is confused and full of random thoughts, and the clock is ticking down faster than you would like. Calm down and maintain the pace that you have set for yourself. Especially as you get down to the last few minutes of the test, don't let the small numbers on the clock make you panic. As long as you are on track by monitoring your pace, you are guaranteed to have time for each question.

⊘ DON'T RUSH

It is very easy to make errors when you are in a hurry. Maintaining a fast pace in answering questions is pointless if it makes you miss questions that you would have gotten right otherwise. Test writers like to include distracting information and wrong answers that seem right. Taking a little extra time to avoid careless mistakes can make all the difference in your test score. Find a pace that allows you to be confident in the answers that you select.

⊘ Keep Moving

Panicking will not help you pass the test, so do your best to stay calm and keep moving. Taking deep breaths and going through the answer elimination steps you practiced can help to break through a stress barrier and keep your pace.

Final Notes

The combination of a solid foundation of content knowledge and the confidence that comes from practicing your plan for applying that knowledge is the key to maximizing your performance on test day. As your foundation of content knowledge is built up and strengthened, you'll find that the strategies included in this chapter become more and more effective in helping you quickly sift through the distractions and traps of the test to isolate the correct answer.

Now that you're preparing to move forward into the test content chapters of this book, be sure to keep your goal in mind. As you read, think about how you will be able to apply this information on the test. If you've already seen sample questions for the test and you have an idea of the question format and style, try to come up with questions of your own that you can answer based on what you're reading. This will give you valuable practice applying your knowledge in the same ways you can expect to on test day.

Good luck and good studying!

Institutions (National, State, and Local)

Governing Systems

Representative Democracy

In a system of government characterized as a **representative democracy**, voters elect representatives to act in their interests. Typically, a **representative** is elected by and responsible to a specific subset of the total population of eligible voters; this subset of the electorate is referred to as a representative's **constituency**. A representative democracy may foster a more powerful legislature than other forms of government systems; to compensate for a strong legislature, most constitutions stipulate that measures must be taken to balance the powers within government, such as the creation of a separate judicial branch. Representative democracy became popular in postindustrial nations where increasing numbers of people expressed an interest in politics but where technology and census counts remained incompatible with systems of direct democracy. Today, the majority of the world's population resides in representative democracies, including constitutional monarchies that possess a strong representative branch.

Anarchism

Anarchism is a philosophy that is synonymous with **anti-authoritarianism**. Many people wrongly associate anarchism with chaos, but in fact, anarchists embrace political philosophies and social movements that support the abolition of government and social hierarchy. In a system that is based on **anarchism**, political and economic institutions would not exist. Rather, individual and community relationships would be voluntary, and people would strive towards a society based on autonomy and freedom. On the one hand, anarchists oppose coercive institutions and social hierarchies, and on the other, they advocate a positive conception of how a voluntary society could work. As with many political ideologies, there are many factions that fall under the umbrella of anarchism that hold varying opinions of how anarchism should be defined. For instance, some anarchists support the use of violence to promote their ideology, while others do not.

Authoritarianism

Authoritarian regimes enforce strong, even oppressive, measures against individuals that fall within their sphere of influence; they often arise when a governing body presumes that it knows what is right for a nation and enforces it. They are typically led by an elite group that employs repressive measures to maintain power, and they do not generally make efforts to gain the consent of individuals or permit feedback on their policies. Under an **authoritarian** government, people are often subject to **government control** over aspects of their lives that in many other systems would be considered personal matters. There is a spectrum of authoritarian ideologies. Examples of authoritarian regimes include absolute monarchies and dictatorships. Democracies can also exhibit authoritarian characteristics in some situations, such as efforts to promote national security. Authoritarian governments typically extend broad-reaching powers to law enforcement bodies, sometimes resulting in a police state; they may or may not have a rule of law and are often corrupt.

Totalitarianism

Totalitarianism is a form of authoritarian political system in which the government **regulates** practically every aspect of public and private conduct. Under **totalitarianism**, individuals and institutions are enveloped into the state's ideology, and the government imposes its political authority by exercising absolute and centralized control over all aspects of life. Individuals are subordinate to the state, and opposition to political and cultural expression is suppressed.

Totalitarian regimes do not tolerate activities by individuals or groups that are not geared toward achieving the state's goals and maintaining the state's ideology. A totalitarian regime maintains power via the use of secret police, propaganda disseminated through government-controlled media, regulation and restriction of free speech, and the use of terror tactics.

COMMUNISM

Communism is a form of an authoritarian, or in some cases totalitarian, political system. A communist country is governed by a single political party that upholds the principles of **Marxism-Leninism**. The goal of communism is to dissolve the state into a **classless society**. According to Marxism, a communist state is one in which the resources and means of production are communally owned rather than individually owned and which provides for equal sharing of all freedoms, work, and benefits. Marxism argues that socialism is a necessary intermediate phase in achieving communism. Therefore, states that are governed by a communist party are actually socialist states and not true communist states, since a true communist state could not exist given the goal of elimination of the state. Historically, communist states have often arisen during political instability. Within communist states, there have rarely been restrictions on state power, resulting in state structures that are totalitarian or authoritarian. Marxist-Leninist ideology views any restriction on state power as an interference in the goal of reaching communism.

FASCISM

Fascism is an authoritarian political ideology and defined the form of rule in Italy from 1922 to 1943 under the leadership of **Mussolini**. Fascism is characterized by efforts to exert state control over all aspects of life, to hold the nation and political party above the individual, and to hold the state as supreme. Fascism also emphasizes loyalty to a single leader and submission to a single nationalistic culture. Fascists support **corporatism** as an economic system, in which economic and social interests of diverse individuals are combined with the interests of the state.

AUTOCRACY, ABSOLUTISM, DESPOTISM, AND DICTATORSHIP

Autocracy is a form of a political system in which unlimited power is held by a single person. **Absolutism** is a form of autocratic political system. Absolutists believe that one person should hold all power. Historically, a monarch ruled in a system characterized as absolutist. Some people believed that an absolute ruler was chosen by God; in this case, opposition against the monarch was equivalent to opposition to God. Therefore, rule was considered absolute in the sense that the ruler could not be challenged. **Despotism** is another form of autocratic political system, characterized as having a government overseen by a single authority that wields absolute power; the authority could be either an individual or a group. A **dictatorship** is a form of absolute rule by a leader, referred to as a dictator, who is unrestricted by law, constitutions, or other social and political forces. Dictatorships are typically associated with single-party states, military regimes, and other forms of authoritarianism.

MONARCHY

Monarchy is one of the oldest forms of government and is defined as an autocratic system in which a monarch serves as **Head of State**. In such a system, the monarch holds office for life. Also included in a monarchy are the individuals and institutions that comprise the royal establishment. In **elective monarchies**, monarchs are appointed to their position for life; in most instances, elective monarchies have been succeeded by **hereditary monarchies**. In a hereditary monarchy, the title of monarch is inherited according to a line of succession; typically one family can trace its origin along a dynasty or bloodline. Most monarchs represent merely a symbol of continuity and statehood, rather than actually serving as a participant in partisan politics. The practice of choosing a monarch varies between countries. A **constitutional monarchy** is one in which the rule of succession is typically established by a law passed by a representative body.

Patriarchy and Tyranny

A patriarchy is a form of autocratic system in which the male members of society tend to hold positions of power. In such a system, the more powerful a position is, the more likely it is that a male will hold that position. **Patriarchy** also describes systems that are characterized as having male leadership in certain hierarchical churches or religious bodies. **Tyranny** is also a form of autocratic system, in which an individual described as a tyrant possesses and wields absolute power and rules by tyranny. Tyrants are typically characterized as cruel despots that place greater significance on their own interests or the interests of a small group of individuals than on the interests of the population and the state that they govern.

Democracy

Democracy, or **rule by the people**, is a form of government in which power is vested in the people and in which policy decisions are made by the majority in a decision-making process such as an election that is open to all or most citizens. Definitions of democracy have become more generalized and include aspects of society and political culture in democratic societies that do not necessarily represent a form of government. What defines a democracy varies, but some of the characteristics of a democracy could include the presence of a middle class, the presence of a civil society, a free market, political pluralism, universal suffrage, and specific rights and freedoms. In practice, however, democracies do have limits on specific freedoms, which are justified as being necessary to maintain democracy and ensure democratic freedoms. For example, freedom of association is limited in democracies for individuals and groups that pose a threat to government or to society.

Parliamentary System

A parliamentary system is a representative democratic system in which the executive branch of government is dependent on the support of a **parliament**. In this system, there is no obvious separation of powers between the executive and legislative branches. However, **parliamentary systems** are generally flexible and responsive to the public. They are characterized as having both a head of government, who is typically the prime minister, and a head of state, who is often a symbol possessing only ceremonial powers. Some parliamentary systems also have an elected president. The features of a parliamentary system include an executive cabinet, headed by the head of government. The cabinet can be removed by the parliament by a vote of no confidence, and likewise, the parliament can be dissolved by the executive.

Presidential/Congressional System

In a presidential system, also referred to as a **congressional system**, the legislative branch and the executive branch are elected separately. The features of a **presidential system** include a president who serves as both the head of state and the head of the government, who has no formal relationship with the legislative branch, who is not a voting member, who cannot introduce bills, and who has a fixed term of office. Elections are held at scheduled times. The president's cabinet carries out the policies of the executive branch and the legislative branch.

Oligarchy

Oligarchy, or **rule by the few**, is a form of political system in which the majority of political power is held by a small portion of society. This power usually resides with the most powerful individuals or groups, such as those that possess wealth, military might, or political influence. Oftentimes, **oligarchies** are comprised of a few powerful families, in which power is passed on from one generation to the next. Members of oligarchies may not wield their power openly but may instead exercise power from behind the scenes, particularly through economic measures.

Aristocracy, Meritocracy, and Plutocracy

Aristocracy is a form of oligarchic system in which the government is led by a ruling class that is considered, either by themselves or by others, to be superior to other members of society. **Meritocracy**, or rule by those who most deserve to rule, is a system that is more flexible than an aristocracy. In a meritocracy, rulers are not automatically considered the best rulers for life but must demonstrate their abilities and achievements in order to maintain power. A **plutocracy** is a system of government led by the wealthy. There is often an overlap between the classification of a government as an aristocracy and a plutocracy, because wealth can enable individuals to portray their own qualities and merits as the best.

A Republic

A republic is a state in which supreme power rests with **citizens** who vote to elect representatives to be responsible to them. The organization of government in a **republic** can vary. In most republics, the head of state is referred to as the president, and in a democratic republic, the head of state is chosen in an election. In some countries, the constitution restricts the number of terms that an individual can serve as president. In the United States, where the head of state is also the head of government, the system is known as a **presidential system**.

Federal Republic

A federal republic is a state that defines itself as both a federation and a republic. A **federation** is a state that is made up of multiple self-governing regions that are united by a central, federal government. The self-government of independent states is guaranteed by a constitution and is not able to be repealed by the central government. Three countries currently characterize themselves as **federal republics**: the Federal Republic of Germany, the Federal Republic of Nigeria, and the Federal Democratic Republic of Ethiopia.

Commonwealth

A commonwealth is a state that is founded on law and united by a compact or by an agreement made by its citizens for the common good of the entire state and for the citizens of the state. In a **commonwealth**, supreme authority is held by the **people**. In the United States, the state of Kentucky, the state of Massachusetts, the state of Pennsylvania, and the state of Virginia are all classified as commonwealths. The term *commonwealth* is also used to describe Puerto Rico and the Northern Marianas Islands, which are both self-governing, autonomous political units that voluntarily associate themselves with the United States of America.

Socialist Republic

In a socialist republic, the constitution or other political doctrine stipulates that the republic operates under a **socialist economic system**, such as a Marxist system. Some **socialist republics** are under the power of a party whose platform is founded on communist ideology, and as such, are referred to as communist states by Western nations. Examples of republics that use the term socialist in their names include the Democratic Socialist Republic of Sri Lanka and the Socialist Republic of Vietnam. Some countries that define themselves as socialist republics, such as India and Guyana, do so in their constitutions rather than in their names. Other countries that identify themselves as socialist republics include North Korea, the People's Republic of China, and Cuba.

Theocracy

A theocracy is a form of a government system in which **religion** or **faith** plays a significant role in the way that the government is run. Commonly, in countries that identify themselves as a **theocracy**, civil rulers are also the leaders of the dominant religion. In these countries, government policies are often strongly guided by religion. Usually, a theocratic government makes a claim to rule on behalf of God or another higher power. The administrative hierarchy of the government often serves as the administrative hierarchy of the dominant religion as well.

Tribalism

Tribalism was the first social system that humans created and coexisted in. It is a system in which society is divided into relatively independent groups referred to as **tribes**. In such a society, tribes themselves have some level of organizational structure, but there is generally very little organization between tribes. Tribes are typically characterized by simple internal organization and structure, with very few differences in social status between individuals. Some tribes nurture the belief that all individuals are equal, and many tribes do not embrace the concept of private property.

Economic System

An economic system addresses the production, distribution, and consumption of goods and services within society and focuses on solving the economic problems of the allocation and scarcity of resources. The composition of an **economic system** consists of people and institutions and the relationships between them. The three questions that must be answered in an economic system are 1) **what** to produce, 2) **how** to produce it, and 3) **for whom** to produce. There are many different types of economic systems, which are often associated with particular ideologies and political systems. Examples of economic systems include market economies, mixed economies, planned economies, traditional economies, and participatory economies.

Capitalism

Capitalism is an economic system in which the means of production are **privately owned**; in which the investment of capital, and the production, distribution and prices of goods and services are determined in a **free market**, and in which the goal of production is to generate **profits**. The features of a **capitalist economic system** include a private sector, private property, free enterprise, and profit. Other features of a capitalist economic system include unequal distribution of wealth, competition, self-organization, the existence of markets, the existence of both a bourgeoisie class and a proletariat class, and the pursuit of self-interest.

Feudalism

Feudalism is a political and economic system that was in existence in Europe from the 9th century through the 15th century. **Feudalism** in the Medieval Age was based on the relationships between lords and vassals and fiefs. A **lord** was a person who held a title of nobility and who owned land. A **vassal** was an individual who was loaned a piece of land by a lord. The piece of land that was owned by the lord and loaned to the vassal was referred to as a **fief**. In exchange for being loaned the fief, the vassal provided military service to the lord.

Socialism

Socialism refers to an economic system in which the means of production and the distribution of goods and services are owned **collectively** or are owned by a **centralized government** that often plans and controls the economy. In practice, **socialism** also refers to the economic phase in **Marxist-Leninist theory** that falls somewhere between capitalism and communism, in which collective ownership of the economy by the proletariat, or the working class, has not yet been achieved. The goal of a socialist economic system is to achieve collective ownership and, ultimately, to achieve a **classless society**.

Mixed Economy

A mixed economy is an economic system blending capitalism and socialism. Such a system is characterized by both private economic freedom and by centralized economic planning. The majority of Western countries, including the United States, have a **mixed economy**. Features of a mixed economy include the freedoms to possess means of production, to travel, to buy and sell, to hire and fire, to organize labor unions or associations, the freedom of communication, and the freedom to protest peacefully. In addition, mixed economies typically provide legal assistance, libraries, roads, schools, hospitals, protection of person and property both at home and abroad, subsidies to agriculture and other businesses, and government monopolies and government-granted monopolies, all of which are funded by taxes or subsidies. There are provisions for autonomy over personal finances, but mixed economies also include socially oriented involuntary spending programs such as welfare, social security, and government subsidies for businesses. Mixed economies also impose environmental, labor, consumer, antitrust, intellectual property, corporate, and import and export laws, as well as taxes and fees.

Colonialism and Imperialism

Colonialism is a political and economic system that is defined as the extension of a nation's sovereignty over territory and people outside its own boundaries, often amounting to the exploitation of a weaker country by a relatively stronger country. Most often, the stronger country is interested in the use of the weaker country's resources, including labor, to strengthen and enrich itself. **Colonialism** also refers to the set of beliefs and values that is used to validate and advance this system, particularly the belief that the culture and civilization of the relatively stronger colonizing country are superior to those of the relatively weaker colonized country. **Imperialism** is a policy of extending control or authority over foreign countries via territorial acquisition or by the establishment of economic and political control over other countries.

Review Video: An Overview of American Imperialism
Visit mometrix.com/academy and enter code: 629170

Neocolonialism

Neocolonialism is a political and economic system in which a **powerful country** uses economic and political measures to extend or continue its influence over **less developed countries**. The term was devised to describe circumstances at the international level after the fall of European colonial empires in the 19th and 20th centuries, particularly the phenomenon of countries and multinational corporations seeking control over other countries through indirect means, such as economic policies, as opposed to the direct military-political control that traditional colonial powers sought. Many people argue that economic tools, such as restrictions on trade and embargos, that are employed by stronger, more developed countries in their relations with less developed countries are reminiscent of colonial power.

Command/Planned Economy

A planned economy is an economic system in which decisions about the production, allocation, and consumption of goods and services are planned in advance; planning can be carried out in either a centralized or decentralized approach. In most **planned economies**, the plans are carried out by means of commands; therefore, planned economies are also commonly referred to as **command economies**. An economic system that is centrally planned by a government is generally referred to as economic statism. Economic statism, by definition, is the practice of giving a centralized government control over economic planning and policy.

Nazism

Nazism was the ideology of the National Socialist German Workers Party (which was led by **Adolf Hitler** in Nazi Germany from 1933 to 1945) during the **Third Reich**. Followers of **Nazism** believed that the Aryan race was superior to other races, and promoted Germanic racial supremacy and a strong, centrally governed state. Nazism is illegal in modern Germany, but small factions of Neo-Nazis continue to exist both in Germany and abroad. Nazis believed that military power would produce a strong nation, opposed multilingualism and multiculturalism, and sought the unification of all German-speaking individuals. Qualities of Nazism included racism; anti-Semitism; the desire for the creation of a master race; anti-Slavism; the belief in the superiority of the White, Germanic, Aryan, or Nordic races; anti-Marxism, anti-Communism, and anti-Bolshevism; rejection of democracy; social Darwinism; eugenics; environmental protection; rejection of the modern art movement and an embrace of classical art; and defense of the Nazi flag.

Police State

A police state is a form of a **totalitarian political system**. A nation does not identify itself as a police state; rather, the characterization is applied by critics of the nation. A **police state** is regulated by police, who exercise power on behalf of an executive authority. It is very difficult to challenge the police and question their conduct in a police state, and there is no rule of law; the law is simply the will of the leader. The police state is based on the concept of enlightened despotism, under which the leader exercises absolute power with the goal of providing for the good of a nation; opposition to government policy is an offense against authority and, therefore, against the nation itself.

Because public dissent is not allowed, people who oppose the government must do so in secret. Therefore, the police must resort to the use of informers and secret police to seek out dissenters.

Westminster System

The Westminster system is a form of **representative democracy**, modeled after the system used in the United Kingdom's Palace of Westminster, where the UK Parliament is located. Features of the **Westminster system** include an executive branch comprised of members of the legislature; a Cabinet made up of senior members of the executive branch; the existence of opposition parties; an elected legislature or a system comprised of two houses, one of which is elected and the other of which is appointed; and a ceremonial head of state, who is distinct from the head of government, and who may hold reserve powers that are not usually exercised. Members of parliament are elected by popular vote, and the head of government is selected via an invitation from the head of state to establish an administration. The head of government, referred to as the **prime minister**, must control a majority of seats within the lower house of parliament or must ensure that there is no absolute majority against them.

Domestic Policy and Foreign Policy

Domestic policy entails all government policy decisions, laws, programs, plans, actions, and behaviors that address **internal state matters**. Examples of **domestic policy** include tax policy, social security and welfare programs, environmental laws and regulations, and regulations on businesses and their practices. In contrast, **foreign policy** addresses how a country will **engage with other countries**. Foreign policy is typically created to protect and promote a country's national interests, national security, ideological goals, and economic prosperity. Foreign policy can be directed toward peaceful cooperation with other countries, as well as towards aggression, war, or exploitation. The creation of foreign policy is typically the responsibility of a country's head of government and foreign minister. In the US, the legislature also has substantial power and influence, which is reflected in the authority of Congress to pass **Foreign Relations Authorization bills**.

United States Federal Government Executive Branch

Term of Appointment and Qualifications for US President

The **President of the United States** is elected for a term of four years. The President may serve for a maximum of two terms. In order to be the President of the United States of America, an individual must be a natural-born citizen of the United States. Candidates for the position of United States President must also be at least thirty-five years of age. Finally, in order to become President of the United States of America, an individual must have been a resident of the United States for at least fourteen years.

Powers of the President of the United States

The President of the US is the Head of the **Executive Branch**. The powers of the President are defined by the US Constitution, and include the power to act as **Commander in Chief of US Armed Forces**; as such, the President can authorize the use of troops without a declaration of war. To declare war, the President must receive approval from Congress. The President must also receive the consent of Congress when using the power to make treaties, appoint the heads of Executive Branch departments, and appoint ambassadors, Supreme Court judges, federal judges, and other officials. The President also has the power to receive foreign ambassadors and other representatives of foreign nations, to provide a yearly State of the Union Address, to recommend legislation, to convene and adjourn Congress, to ensure that laws are carried out, to fill administrative openings when Congress is in recess, and to issue reprieves and pardons for crimes against the United States.

Legislative Powers of the President

The President can **recommend legislation** to members of Congress, who can then introduce it as a bill. Only Congress can create legislation, but the President's approval of a bill is significant in determining whether it will pass. The President may sign a bill into law, veto a bill, or do nothing with it once it has passed Congress and been sent to the President for approval. If the President **signs a bill into law**, only the Supreme Court can then dismiss it by finding it unconstitutional. If a bill is **vetoed**, it is sent back to Congress without the President's signature, where Congress can override the veto with two-thirds approval. If the President does nothing with a bill, and Congress is in session ten business days following the receipt of the bill by the President, it becomes **law** without the President's signature; if Congress adjourns within ten business days, the bill dies, which is referred to as a **pocket veto**. The President can only veto a bill in its entirety.

Review Video: Executive Branch
Visit mometrix.com/academy and enter code: 210629

Secretary of Agriculture and the Department of Agriculture

The Secretary of Agriculture is a member of the President's Cabinet and is the head of the **Department of Agriculture**, which was established in 1862. The Department of Agriculture is responsible for efforts to maintain and increase agricultural profits, as well as efforts to foster international markets for United States agricultural products. One of the purposes of the Department of Agriculture is to aid in alleviating poverty, hunger, and malnutrition. Another goal of the Department of Agriculture is to improve agricultural production by aiding in the protection of natural resources. The Department of Agriculture is responsible for ensuring the quality and safety of food by the use of inspection and grading activities.

Presidential Impeachment

By definition, impeachment is the first step in the process of **removing an official from office** by a charge of crime or misconduct while in office. In the case of the President of the United States, if the **House of Representatives** believes that the President has committed criminal activity or engaged in misconduct while in office, specifically treason, bribery, and other high crimes and misdemeanors, the House can **impeach** the President by majority vote. After the House has impeached the President, the **Senate** examines the case and votes to convict the President or not. If two-thirds of the Senate votes to convict the President, he is removed from his position. The process of impeachment is overseen by the **Chief Justice of the Supreme Court**.

President's Budget

The **Budget and Accounting Act of 1921** requires the President to submit an annual document to Congress by the first Monday of February containing the proposed spending plan for the Federal Government in the upcoming fiscal year. The budget is essentially a set of goals with associated costs. The purpose of the budget is to provide a guide for Congress to use when determining how much money to spend, what to spend money on, and how to raise money to meet spending goals. The **Office of Management and Budget** helps the President with the annual spending plan. Federal appropriations must be approved by Congress. When Congress receives the spending plan, the House of Representatives establishes a **level of spending** for the Federal Government. Finally, Congress determines how this level of spending will be allocated for various Federal actions.

President's Cabinet

The President's Cabinet is comprised of the heads of the executive departments, who **advise** the President on issues related to their respective departments on a weekly basis. Members of the **Cabinet** include the Vice President, the Attorney General, and the Secretaries of Agriculture, Commerce, Defense, Education, Energy, Health and Human Services, Homeland Security, Housing and Urban Development, Interior, Labor, State, Transportation, Treasury, and Veterans Affairs. Department heads are appointed by the President and confirmed by a majority vote in the Senate. They remain in their positions for the length of the President's administration, and when a new administration begins, the heads of the executive departments are expected to leave their positions. The President can fire the head of an executive department without approval from Congress.

Secretary of State

The Secretary of State is a member of the President's Cabinet and is the head of the **Department of State**, which was established in 1789. The Department of State is responsible for advising the President on foreign policy, implementing foreign policy, and working on behalf of American interests internationally. The Department of State works with citizens of the United States, Congress, other departments and agencies within the United States government, and foreign governments. The Department of State is responsible for negotiating international treaties and agreements and representing the United States in international organizations, including the United Nations, and at international meetings.

Secretary of the Treasury and the Department of the Treasury

The Secretary of the Treasury is a member of the President's Cabinet and is the head of the **Department of the Treasury**, which was established in 1789. The Department of the Treasury is responsible for developing and recommending economic, financial, tax, and fiscal policies, acting as the US government's primary financial agent, enforcing laws, and producing coins and currency. The **Secretary of the Treasury** is the President's key advisor on national and international **financial, economic, and tax policy**. The Secretary of the Treasury also assists with developing wide-ranging economic policies and handles public debt.

Secretary of Defense and the Department of Defense

The Secretary of Defense is a member of the President's Cabinet and is the head of the **Department of Defense**, which was established in 1947. The Department of Defense is responsible for protecting United States security by supplying **armed forces**. The armed forces of the United States are comprised of the Army, Navy, Marine Corps, and Air Force. The Reserve and National Guard also exist as part of the Department of Defense to assist in case of emergency. The Defense Department is also staffed by civilian employees. The **Secretary of Defense** is responsible for directing and overseeing the Department of Defense.

Attorney General and the Department of Justice

The Attorney General is a member of the President's Cabinet and is the head of the **Department of Justice**, which was established in 1870. The Department of Justice is responsible for providing legal counsel for the people of the United States. The Department of Justice consists of lawyers, investigators, and federal agents. The **Attorney General** is responsible for directing the Department of Justice, and in rare circumstances will represent the United States government in Supreme Court cases. The Attorney General also advises the President and the other heads of the executive departments on **legal matters**.

Secretary of the Interior and the Department of the Interior

The Secretary of the interior is a member of the President's Cabinet and is the head of the **Department of the Interior**, which was established in 1849. The Department of the Interior is responsible for protecting and ensuring access to the **natural and cultural resources** of the United States. The Department of the Interior is also responsible for ensuring that the United States upholds its responsibilities to Native American tribes. The Department of the Interior administers the public lands and minerals, national parks, national wildlife refuges, and western water resources of the United States. The employees of the Department of the Interior work on issues related to migratory wildlife conservation, historic preservation, endangered species, and the protection and restoration of lands that have undergone surface mining, mapping, and geological, hydrological, and biological sciences.

Secretary of Commerce and the Department of Commerce

The Secretary of Commerce is a member of the President's Cabinet and is the head of the **Department of Commerce**, which was established in 1903. The Department of Commerce is responsible for furthering international trade, economic growth, and technological advancement opportunities for the United States. The Department of Commerce works to increase the competitiveness of the United States in the international economy and decrease unfair competition in international trade. The Department of Commerce also conducts social and economic statistical analysis; conducts science, engineering, and technology research; and makes efforts to advance knowledge and utilization of the physical environment and ocean resources. In addition, the Department of Commerce issues patents and trademarks. The Department of Commerce also researches and makes policies related to telecommunications, aids in fostering domestic economic growth, and works to further the development of minority-owned businesses.

The **Secretary of Commerce** advises the President on issues pertaining to the **industrial and commercial areas** of the United States economy.

Secretary of Labor and the Department of Labor

The Secretary of Labor is a member of the President's Cabinet and is the head of the **Department of Labor**, which was established in 1913. The Department of Labor is responsible for advancing the well-being of workers in the United States, bettering working conditions, and increasing the employment opportunities available to workers. To meet these responsibilities, the Department of Labor administers **Federal labor laws** to ensure the rights of employees to a safe working environment, a minimum wage, overtime pay, unemployment insurance, and workers' compensation. The Department of Labor also administers labor laws to ensure that discrimination does not occur in the workplace. Other efforts that the Department of Labor makes in the interest of workers involve the protection of employee pension rights, job training programs, job placement programs, improving collective bargaining ability, and monitoring economic indicators related to employment.

Secretary and Department of Health and Human Services

The Secretary of Health and Human Services is a member of the President's Cabinet and is the head of the **Department of Health and Human Services**, which was established in 1953. The Department of Health and Human Services is responsible for protecting the health of the citizens of the United States and providing vital human services. The Department of Health and Human Services conducts health and social science research, conducts research aimed at preventing disease, researches and provides immunization services, works to ensure food and drug safety, manages Medicare and Medicaid, provides health information technology, provides financial aid and services for low-income families, works to better maternal and infant health, manages the program Head Start for pre-school students, supports community programs, works to reduce child abuse and domestic violence, supports substance abuse treatment and prevention, supports services for the elderly, ensures health services for Native Americans, and prepares for medical emergencies. The **Secretary of Health and Human Services** provides advice to the President on issues regarding **health, welfare, and income security**.

Housing and Urban Development and the Department of Housing

The Secretary of Housing and Urban Development is a member of the President's Cabinet and is the head of the **Department of Housing and Urban Development**, which was established in 1965. The Department of Housing and Urban Development is responsible for developing programs and policies related to **housing and community development** in the United States. Specifically, the Department of Housing and Urban Development administers housing assistance programs, fosters state and local involvement in addressing housing and community development issues, and promotes donations from private house building and mortgage lending companies to housing and community development programs.

Secretary of Transportation and the Department of Transportation

The Secretary of Transportation is a member of the President's Cabinet and is the head of the **Department of Transportation**, which was established in 1966. The Department of Transportation is responsible for developing **transportation policy** in the United States, including with relation to highway planning, development, and construction, mass transportation in urban areas, railroads, aviation, and the safety and security of the waterways, ports, highways, and oil and gas pipelines of the United States. The Department of Transportation develops transportation policy in coordination with state and local agencies and organizations. Transportation policies greatly impact other sectors, including land management, resource conservation, and technology.

Secretary of Energy and the Department of Energy

The Secretary of Energy is a member of the President's Cabinet and is the head of the **Department of Energy**, which was established in 1977. The Department of Energy is responsible for developing and sharing technical, scientific, and educational information with leaders and policy-makers in order to foster efficient energy consumption, the development and implementation of a wide variety of energy sources, economic production and competition, higher standards of environmental quality, and a secure and stable defense program for the United States.

Secretary of Education and the Department of Education

The Secretary of Education is a member of the President's Cabinet and is the head of the **Department of Education**, which was established in 1979. The Department of Education is responsible for developing policies and administering federal assistance for **educational programs**. The goal of the Department of Education is to provide equal access to education for all citizens of the United States and to foster quality educational programs. The Secretary of Education provides advice to the President related to education policies and programs.

Secretary of Veterans Affairs and the Department of Veterans Affairs

The Secretary of Veterans Affairs is a member of the President's Cabinet and is the head of the **Department of Veterans Affairs**, which was established in 1988. The Department of Veterans Affairs is responsible for administering programs with the goal of providing benefits to veterans and their families. Specifically, the Department of Veterans Affairs provides funds for disabilities or death that results from military service, pensions, educational benefits, rehabilitation benefits, home loan guaranties, burial benefits, and a healthcare program that encompasses nursing homes, clinics, and medical centers for veterans. The Department of Veterans Affairs is made up of the **Veterans Health Administration**, the **Veterans Benefits Administration**, and the **National Cemetery Administration**, each of which has a central office and field offices.

Secretary of Homeland Security and the Department of Homeland Security

The Secretary of Homeland Security is a member of the President's Cabinet and is the head of the **Department of Homeland Security**, which was established in 2003. The Department of Homeland Security is responsible for efforts aimed at preventing **terrorist attacks** against the United States. The Department of Homeland Security is also responsible for efforts to reduce the susceptibility of the United States to terrorism. In addition, the Department of Homeland Security is responsible for efforts aimed at reducing the devastation and suffering from potential terrorist attacks and natural disasters.

Presidential Succession Act of 1947

The Presidential Succession Act of 1947 specifies the order of **succession** if the President of the United States is unable to carry out the duties and responsibilities of the office of the President due to death, resignation, removal from office, or due to conditions that otherwise render the President incapacitated. In such a situation, the office of the President will be filled by the following people, in order: Vice President, Speaker of the House, President Pro Tempore of the Senate, Secretary of State, Secretary of the Treasury, Secretary of Defense, Attorney General, Secretary of the Interior, Secretary of Agriculture, Secretary of Commerce, Secretary of Labor, Secretary of Health and Human Services, Secretary of Housing and Urban Development, Secretary of Transportation, Secretary of Energy, Secretary of Education, Secretary of Veterans Affairs, and finally Secretary of Homeland Security.

United States Federal Government Judicial Branch

Judicial Branch

The United States Judicial Branch was established with the creation of the US Supreme Court, which was stipulated by **Article III** of the US Constitution. The **Supreme Court** is the highest court in the United States, and it is granted the judicial powers of the United States government. In addition to the Supreme Court, the judicial branch also consists of lower **Federal courts** that were created by Congress using its Constitutional powers. The responsibility of the Courts is to settle disputes about the meaning of laws and how laws are applied, and, through **judicial review**, to decide whether or not laws violate the US Constitution. It is through judicial review that the judicial branch exercises the system of checks and balances with regard to the executive and legislative branches.

Review Video: Duties of the Judicial Branch
Visit mometrix.com/academy and enter code: 278093

Powers of the Supreme Court

The **Supreme Court** is tasked with settling disputes involving the interpretation of the **Constitution**. The process of determining whether a law or action is in violation of the Constitution is **judicial review**. The Supreme Court can overturn both state and federal laws if they are determined to violate the Constitution. The decisions of the Supreme Court can only be altered by means of another Supreme Court decision or through an amendment to the Constitution. The Supreme Court has full authority over federal courts and restricted authority over state courts. The Supreme Court has the final say over cases heard by federal courts and also stipulates the procedures that federal courts must abide by. Although federal courts are required to uphold the Supreme Court's interpretations of federal laws and the Constitution and the Supreme Court's interpretations of federal law and the Constitution also apply to state courts, the Supreme Court cannot interpret state laws or Constitutions and doesn't oversee state court procedures.

Supreme Court Justices

Nine Justices currently comprise the Supreme Court; eight of these are referred to as **Associate Justices** and one is referred to as the **Chief Justice**. The number of Supreme Court Justices is set by Congress. The Supreme Court Justices are appointed by the President of the United States and with consent from the Senate. After individuals have been approved by the Senate and have been sworn in to the Supreme Court, they may keep the position of Supreme Court Justice for the remainder of their lives. Justices may leave their positions if they choose to resign or retire, or if they die, or if they are impeached. Historically, there has never been a Justice who has been removed from the Supreme Court through impeachment. There are not any specific requirements to become a Supreme Court Justice.

Appealing Cases in Higher Courts

Prior to being heard before the Supreme Court, cases are typically first heard before **lower courts**, including both state and federal courts. If a lower court makes a decision that the losing party in the case believes is unjust, that party has the option of appealing the case and bringing it before a higher court. At the state level, courts where appeals are heard are referred to as **appellate courts**. At the federal level, lower courts are referred to as **United States District Courts** and higher courts are referred to as **United States Courts of Appeals**.

Supreme Court and Original Jurisdiction

Although it is rare for cases to originate in the Supreme Court, it does have the power of **original jurisdiction** to hear cases involving ambassadors and other foreign officials. Similarly, cases involving two or more states originate in the Supreme Court. If a decision made by a higher court is in disagreement with a decision made by a lower court, the decision made by the lower court is **overturned**. If a decision made by a higher court is in agreement with a decision made by a lower court, the losing party can request that the case be heard before the **Supreme Court**. However, only cases addressing federal or Constitutional law are heard before the Supreme Court.

Bringing A Case before the Supreme Court

The total number of cases sent to the Supreme Court annually is around 7,500. However, the Supreme Court typically only hears between eighty and one hundred of these cases. When a case is submitted to the Supreme Court, the Supreme Court Justices convene to determine whether the case should be heard before the Court. The criteria used to make this determination specifically include deciding whether the case addresses **federal law** or **Constitutional law**. In addition, the Justices must take into consideration the possibility that any decision made in the Supreme Court could affect the outcome of many cases heard before lower courts and subsequently make efforts to exercise this power only in cases involving a constitutional issue.

Supreme Court Hearing

The Supreme Court is in **session** from the first Monday in October through late June of the following year. If the Justices are not hearing cases, they conduct legal research and write opinions. On Fridays, Justices deliberate cases that they have heard and vote. If the Supreme Court Justices decide to hear a case, legal representation for each side has a half-hour to present an oral argument. Justices may ask questions throughout oral arguments. A majority of the Justices are required to decide a case. If the Chief Justice sides with the majority, he or she writes the **majority opinion**, or the Chief Justice assigns the task to another Justice on the majority side. If the Chief Justice does not side with the majority, the Justice who has served the longest on the Supreme Court writes the opinion or assigns the task to one of the other Justices. Opinions form the foundation for arguments in similar future cases, serving as **precedent**. Justices who are in the minority may write **dissenting opinions**.

Supreme Court Officers

The Supreme Court is aided by Court Officers, who help to ensure that the functions of the court are carried out smoothly. The **Court Officers** include the Administrative Assistant to the Chief Justice, who is appointed by the Chief Justice. In addition, the Court Officers include the Clerk, the Reporter of Decisions, the Librarian, and the Marshal, all of whom are appointed by the Supreme Court. The Court Officers also include the Director of Budget and Personnel, the Court Counsel, the Curator, the Director of Data Systems, and the Public Information Officer. These Court Officers are appointed by the **Chief Justice** with the advice of the rest of the Supreme Court.

Jurisdiction of the Federal Courts

The Constitution stipulates that the federal courts have jurisdiction over cases involving a number of issues. **Federal judicial power** extends to cases involving the United States Constitution, federal laws, and treaties. Federal courts deal with cases involving ambassadors and other foreign officials, cases involving admiralty and maritime issues, cases in which the United States federal government is a party, cases involving disputes between two or more states, cases involving disputes between a state and citizens of another state, cases involving disputes between citizens of different states, cases involving citizens from one state who are claiming land in different states, and cases involving disputes between a state or its citizens and foreign states or foreign citizens. The Supreme Court has **original jurisdiction** in cases involving ambassadors and other foreign ministers and in any case in which a state is a party. In all other cases, the Supreme Court has **appellate jurisdiction**.

Powers Denied and Restrictions on the Federal Government

There are a number of powers that the federal government is not granted. The federal government does not have the power to suspend the **Writ of Habeas Corpus**. The federal government does not have the power to pass a **Bill of Attainder** or an **ex post facto law**. The federal government is restricted from displaying preferential treatment for one state over others. The federal government does not have the power to spend money from the US Treasury before first receiving the approval of Congress. The federal government does not have the power to confer a title of nobility to any individual. An individual who holds a federal government office is restricted from accepting gifts from foreign countries; this restriction exists to prevent offers that might constitute bribes.

How Laws are Made

Part I

Laws can originate in either the House of Representatives or the Senate. When a Congressman wants to propose a new **law**, that person sponsors the **bill** and introduces it to the respective Congressional chamber by either giving it to the clerk or placing it in a special box known as the hopper. A legislative number is assigned to the bill, designated by *H.R.* for bills originating in the House of Representatives or *S.* for bills originating in the Senate. The bill is printed and given to all members of the house. The bill is assigned to a committee for investigation and discussion, which often involves hearings.

Part II

Following an investigation into a proposed bill, the committee releases the bill and recommends that it be passed, recommends that the bill be revised prior to being released, or sets it aside so that it cannot be voted on. If a bill is **released**, it is added to a calendar of bills waiting to be voted on. On the floor of the chamber, the bill is read, and if it passes by a simple majority, it goes to the other congressional house. In order for the bill to be introduced in the other house, a member of that house must **announce the introduction** of it. The same process of being assigned to a committee and investigation is repeated in the second house. If the bill also passes by a simple majority in the second house, it goes to a **conference committee** comprised of members of both houses.

Part III

The **conference committee** reconciles any differences between the two houses with regard to the bill, and if any alterations are made, the committee sends the bill back to each house for final approval. After the bill has been approved, it is **printed**, or **enrolled**, and **certified**. The enrolled bill is then signed by both the Speaker of the House and the Vice President, who is the leader of the Senate. After the bill has received the necessary signatures, it is sent to the President of the United States, where he must sign it within ten days or veto it. If the President **signs** the bill, it becomes law. If the President chooses to **veto** the bill, it is sent back to Congress, and if two-thirds of both houses vote to pass the bill, it becomes law without the President's signature.

Courts of Appeals

The second-highest level of the federal judiciary branch is comprised of the **courts of appeals**. The courts of appeals were created in 1891 to reduce the overwhelming number of cases that were sent to the Supreme Court and more quickly and efficiently process cases. There are twelve **regional circuit courts of appeal**, as well as the **US Court of Appeals for the Federal Circuit**. Most circuit courts have between ten and fifteen judges, but the number varies widely between courts. The purpose of the courts of appeals is to review the decisions of the district courts or of the trial courts at the federal level, and to review orders of regulatory agencies in instances where the agencies have reviewed the orders themselves internally but there remains dissent over legal issues. The Court of Appeals for the Federal Circuit also has national jurisdiction to hear appeals in unique circumstances.

District Courts

The district courts are below the courts of appeals. There are ninety-four **districts** among the fifty states and territories of the US Districts are established by Congress based on the population, the size, and the caseload in a particular area. Small states can represent an entire district; larger states are divided into up to four districts. There are at minimum two judges for every **district court**. Judges must be residents of the district they work in, with the exception of judges in D.C. District courts sessions are held in varying cities within a district for specific durations of time in each city. The types of cases that appear before district courts address issues related to federal crimes. District courts are the only federal courts in which a grand jury indicts individuals accused of criminal acts and a jury makes a decision on a case. In every district, there is also a **US bankruptcy court**, as bankruptcy issues must be handled in federal courts as opposed to state courts.

Special Courts

Occasionally, a need arises to establish a court to meet a particular purpose. Such special courts are referred to as **legislative courts**, as they are established by Congress. In special courts, judges are appointed to life terms, just as judges are in other federal courts. Also, similarly to other federal court judges, special court judges must be appointed by the President of the US and approved by the Senate. There are currently two special trial courts with national jurisdiction. The first is the **Court of International Trade**, which hears cases dealing with international trade and customs concerns. The second is the **US Court of Federal Claims**, which hears cases involving claims for financial damages against the US government, cases involving disputes concerning federal contracts, cases involving situations in which the federal government is accused of unlawfully taking private property, and other cases involving claims against the US government.

United States Federal Government Legislative Branch

Congress

Congress represents one part of the legislative branch in the United States. **Congress** is composed of two chambers known as the **House of Representatives** and the **Senate**. The two-chamber system is referred to as a **bicameral legislative system**. Congress is responsible for writing, debating, and passing **bills**. Once bills are passed by Congress, they go to the President of the United States to be reviewed, approved, and signed into law. Congress is also responsible for investigating issues that are important on a national level and for overseeing both the executive and judicial branches. Elections are held every two years for all 435 members of the House of Representatives and for one-third of the members of the Senate. Congress begins a new session every January after Congressional elections. Congress convenes once a year, typically from January 3rd through July 31st.

Powers of Congress

Article I, Section 8 of the Constitution gives Congress the power to establish and collect taxes, to pay debts, to provide for the defense of the country, to borrow money on credit, to regulate domestic and international commerce, to establish immigration policy, to establish bankruptcies laws, to create money, to establish a postal system, to protect patents and intellectual property rights, to create lower courts, to control and protect citizens and ships in international waters, to declare war, to establish and maintain an army and a navy, to maintain National Guard readiness, and to exercise control over the District of Columbia and other federal property. Section 8 also includes a clause known as the **Elastic Clause**, which gives Congress the power to pass any law necessary for carrying out the actions over which it has power.

LEGISLATIVE BRANCH

The Legislative branch was established by **Article I** of the United States Constitution. The **Legislative branch** is responsible for making laws. In the United States, the Legislative branch is a **bicameral system**, which means that it is divided into two houses, the **House of Representatives** and the **Senate**. The bicameral system ensures that **checks and balances** exist within the Legislative branch. Representatives and Senators are elected by the people in the state that they represent. Also included in the Legislative branch are all of the agencies that provide support to Congress, including the Government Printing Office, the Library of Congress, the Congressional Budget Office, the General Accounting Office, and the Architect of the Capitol.

Review Video: Legislative Branch
Visit mometrix.com/academy and enter code: 405303

Review Video: Bicameral Legislature
Visit mometrix.com/academy and enter code: 756921

COMMITTEE SYSTEM

The Congressional committee system started in 1789. **Congressional committees** are created to address political, social, and economic changes. Both the House and the Senate have their own committees, and there are also **joint committees** between both houses. To address an increasing number of issues that must be discussed, **subcommittees** have also formed. Committees are responsible for investigating each bill that is proposed to Congress. This investigation could include holding hearings where expert witnesses provide information and facts that are relevant to the bill. Once the committee has heard all the facts, it either recommends the bill as it was originally written or it suggests that the bill should be passed with amendments. Occasionally, bills are **tabled**, or put aside, which stops consideration of those bills. Once a bill is passed in each house, a committee called the conference committee works to find common ground between House and Senate versions of the bill. After both houses agree to the same version of the bill and it passes a final vote, it is sent to the President.

HOUSE OF REPRESENTATIVES

There are 435 members of the **House of Representatives**. Every member represents a region within a state; these regions are referred to as congressional districts and are based on population size. Congressional districts are established every ten years through the process of a **population census,** which is carried out by the US Census Bureau. The number of congressional districts in a state determines how many Representatives are from that state. Every state has at least one seat in the House. Representatives come not only from the fifty states but, in addition, five members represent Puerto Rico, Guam, American Samoa, the Virgin Islands, and D.C. These five members are not permitted to vote in Congress but are permitted to engage in debates. The House is solely responsible for initiating laws that require citizens to pay taxes and for determining whether government officials should be tried for committing crimes against the US.

Standing Committees of the House of Representatives

Although Congressional committees are created to address changing political, social, and economic conditions, there are a number of committees that are permanent, known as **standing committees**. The standing committees within the **House of Representatives** include the Agriculture Committee, the Appropriations Committee, the Armed Services Committee, the Banking and Financial Services Committee, the Budget Committee, the Commerce Committee, the Education and the Workforce Committee, the Government Reform and Oversight Committee, the House Administration Committee, the International Relations Committee, the Judiciary Committee, the Resources Committee, the Rules Committee, the Science Committee, the Small Business Committee, the Standards of Official Conduct Committee, the Transportation and Infrastructure Committee, the Veterans' Affairs Committee, and the Ways and Means Committee.

House Committee on Agriculture

The House Committee on Agriculture was established in 1820. The committee has jurisdiction over the degradation of seeds, over the control of insect pests, and over the protection of fauna in forest reserves. The committee also has jurisdiction over agriculture, agricultural and industrial chemistry, agricultural colleges and laboratories, agricultural economics, agricultural education extension services, agricultural production and marketing, prices of agricultural products and commodities, animal industries, animal disease, commodity exchanges, crop insurance, soil conservation, the dairy industry, entomology, plant quarantine, extension of farm credit and farm security, inspection of meat and seafood products, forestry, human nutrition and home economics, plant industry, soils, agricultural engineering, rural electrification, rural development, and water conservation. Subcommittees include the Subcommittee on Conservation, Credit, Rural Development and Research; the Subcommittee on General Farm Commodities and Risk Management; the Subcommittee on Specialty Crops and Foreign Agriculture Programs; the Subcommittee on Department Operations, Oversight, Dairy, Nutrition and Forestry; and the Subcommittee on Livestock and Horticulture.

House Committee on Appropriations

The House Committee on Appropriations was created in 1865. The committee has jurisdiction over the appropriation of money to government departments, the withdrawal of appropriations, and the transfer of unspent funds. The committee holds hearings to review budget recommendations and policies of the President and to review the financial factors used to come up with the budget. Subcommittees of the House Committee on Appropriations include the Subcommittee on Agriculture, Rural Development, Food and Drug Administration, and Related Agencies; the Subcommittee on Defense; the Subcommittee on Energy and Water Development, and Related Agencies; the Subcommittee on Foreign Operations, Export Financing and Related Programs; the Subcommittee on Homeland Security; the Subcommittee on Interior, Environment, and Related Agencies; the Subcommittee on Labor, Health and Human Services, Education, and Related Agencies; the Subcommittee on Military Quality of Life and Veterans Affairs, and Related Agencies; the Subcommittee on Science, the Departments of State, Justice, and Commerce, and Related Agencies; and the Subcommittee on Transportation, Treasury, and Housing and Urban Development, The Judiciary, and District of Columbia.

House Committee on Armed Services

The House Committee on Armed Services has jurisdiction over matters related to defense and the Department of Defense, including the Departments of the Army, Navy and Air Force, ammunition storage facilities, forts, arsenals, and Army, Navy, and Air Force locations. In addition, the committee has jurisdiction over the conservation, cultivation, and use of naval oil reserves, as well as canals connecting oceans, the Merchant Marine Academy, and state Merchant Marine Academies.

The committee also has jurisdiction over nuclear energy as it is applied within the military, tactical intelligence, matters related to the merchant marine that affect national security, the salaries and benefits of individuals who are in the armed forces, scientific R&D for the armed forces, the selective service, the size and makeup of the armed forces, soldiers and sailors homes, and materials required to provide defense. Subcommittees include the Tactical Air and Land Forces Subcommittee; the Readiness Subcommittee; the Terrorism, Unconventional Threats and Capabilities Subcommittee; the Military Personnel Subcommittee; the Strategic Forces Subcommittee; and the Projection Forces Subcommittee.

House Committee on the Budget

The House Committee on the Budget is responsible for developing a budget resolution that establishes spending and revenue levels for federal programs. The committee has oversight over the laws and regulations that are relevant to the **budget process**, as well as over the agencies that hold the responsibility for the administration of such laws. Specifically, the committee has jurisdiction over the Budget and Accounting Act of 1920, the Congressional Budget Act of 1974, and the Emergency Balanced Budget and Deficit Control Act of 1985, and the agencies over which it holds jurisdiction include the Office of Management and Budget and the Congressional Budget Office. The committee also investigates tax expenditures and the impact of legislation on budget expenditures. In addition, the committee has jurisdiction over budget priorities, budget enforcement, budget process reform, and direct spending and tax incentives.

House Committee on Education and the Workforce: Education

The House Committee on Education and the Workforce was created in 1997. The committee has jurisdiction over issues concerning education and labor. All levels of **education** are addressed by the committee, including elementary and secondary education programs, the Every Student Succeeds Act, school choice for low-income individuals, special education, educator quality and educator training, scientific reading instruction, vocational and technical education, higher education programs, college access for low and middle-income individuals, financial aid, early childhood and preschool programs, Head Start, school lunch and nutrition, financial oversight of the US Department of Education, care and treatment of at-risk children, child abuse prevention, child adoption, educational research and advancement, adult education, and anti-poverty programs.

House Committee on Education and the Workforce: Workforce

The House Committee on Education and the Workforce was created in 1997. The committee has jurisdiction over issues concerning education and labor. The committee promotes efforts to improve health care, job training, and retirement security for **workers**. The committee also promotes efforts to advance opportunities for people, especially in the area of emerging knowledge. Specific items on the agenda of the committee with regard to workforce include pension and retirement security for workers, access to health care and other benefits for workers, job training, adult education, and workforce development, welfare reform, protecting democratic rights for union members, health and safety, offering more scheduling and work arrangement choices and flexibility for workers, equal employment opportunity, civil rights, wages and hours of labor, workers' compensation, family and medical leave, the relationships between employers and employees.

House Committee on Energy and Commerce

The House Committee on Energy and Commerce is the longest-standing committee in the House of Representatives. The committee has broad jurisdiction, including jurisdiction over issues pertaining to telecommunications, consumer protection, food and drug safety, public health, air quality, environmental health, supply and delivery of energy, and interstate and foreign commerce. The committee has jurisdiction over the Department of Energy, the Department of Health and Human Services, the Department of Transportation, the Federal Trade Commission, the Food and Drug Administration, and the Federal Communications Commission. Subcommittees of the House Committee on Energy and Commerce include the Subcommittee on Commerce, Trade and Consumer Protection; the Subcommittee on Energy and Air Quality; the Subcommittee on Environment and Hazardous Materials; the Subcommittee on Health; the Subcommittee on Oversight and Investigations; and the Subcommittee on Telecommunications and the Internet.

House Committee on Financial Services

The House Committee on Financial Services has jurisdiction over banks and banking, stabilization of the economy, defense production, commodity, rent, service prices, financial assistance for commerce and industry, insurance, international finance, international financial and monetary organizations, money and credit, public and private housing, securities and exchanges, and urban development. The House Committee on Financial Services has several subcommittees, including the Subcommittee on Capital Markets, Insurance, and Government Sponsored Enterprises; the Subcommittee on Domestic and International Monetary Policy, Trade, and Technology; the Subcommittee on Financial Institutions and Consumer Credit; the Subcommittee on Housing and Community Opportunity; and the Subcommittee on Oversight and Investigations.

House Committee on Government Reform

The House Committee on Government Reform is the most important legislative **investigative and oversight committee**. The committee has oversight over the National Guard, the Reserves, Homeland Security, the US Postal Service, management reform, diploma mills, electronic voting, regulatory affairs, the Bureau of Economic Analysis, the Unfunded Mandates Reform Act, new dietary guidelines, the thrift savings plan, security clearance reform, federal agency contracting, the General Services Administration, information technology and information policy, intellectual property piracy, the Department of the interior's tribal recognition process, D.C., flu vaccine supply and state and local health preparedness, FDA post-marketing surveillance, USDA cattle surveillance, and 21st-century healthcare. There are numerous subcommittees of the House Committee on Government Reform, including the Subcommittee on Criminal Justice, Drug Policy and Human Resources; the Subcommittee on Energy and Resources; the Subcommittee on Federalism and the Census; the Subcommittee on Federal Workforce and Agency Organization; the Subcommittee on Government Management, Finance, and Accountability; the Subcommittee on National Security, Emerging Threats, and International Relations; and the Subcommittee on Regulatory Affairs.

House Committee on Homeland Security

The House Committee on Homeland Security has jurisdiction over a wide spectrum of issues and factors pertaining to the prevention of **terrorist attacks** on the US, particularly involving weapons that are characterized as nuclear and biological weapons. The subcommittees of the Committee on Homeland Security include the Subcommittee on Prevention of Nuclear and Biological Attack; the Subcommittee on Intelligence, Information Sharing, and Terrorism Risk Assessment; the Subcommittee on Economic Security, Infrastructure Protection, and Cybersecurity; the Subcommittee on Management, Integration, and Oversight; the Subcommittee on Emergency Preparedness, Science, and Technology; and the Subcommittee on Investigations.

House Committee on House Administration

The House Committee on House Administration is responsible for overseeing **federal elections** as well as the daily functions of the **House of Representatives**. Specifically, the Committee on House Administration has jurisdiction over the Library of Congress, statues and pictures, the acceptance of or purchase of works of art for the Capitol, and the Botanic Garden. The **Committee on House**

Administration also has jurisdiction over the purchase of books and manuscripts and the Smithsonian Institution. The Committee on House Administration is also responsible for the oversight of the establishment of other institutions similar to the Smithsonian Institution.

House Committee on International Relations

The House Committee on International Relations has jurisdiction over issues pertaining to international relations between the US and other countries, procurement of property for US embassies, the delineation of boundaries between the US and other countries, export controls, nonproliferation of nuclear technology, foreign loans, international commodity agreements, international conferences and congresses, international education, international intervention and war, diplomacy, efforts to promote US commercial interests globally, international economic policy, neutrality, protection of US citizens abroad, the American Red Cross, trading with enemies, and the United Nations. Subcommittees of the House Committee on International Relations include the Subcommittee on Asia and the Pacific; the Subcommittee on Africa, Global Human Rights, and International Operations; the Subcommittee on the Western Hemisphere; the Subcommittee on Europe and Emerging Threats; the Subcommittee on the Middle East and Central Asia; the Subcommittee on Oversight and Investigations; and the Subcommittee on International Terrorism and Nonproliferation.

House Committee on the Judiciary

The House Committee on the Judiciary was created in 1813. The committee has jurisdiction over the judiciary, both civil and criminal judicial proceedings, administrative practices and procedures, the apportionment of Representatives, bankruptcy, mutiny, espionage, counterfeiting, civil liberties, constitutional amendments, criminal law enforcement, federal courts and judges, local courts in US territories and possessions, immigration policy, interstate compacts, cases against the US government, members of Congress, national jails, patents, the Patent and Trademark Office, copyrights, trademarks, succession to the office of President, protection of trade and commerce against illegal obstacles and monopolies, revision and codification of statutes, the boundaries of states and territories, and activities that are considered treacherous and threatening to the security of the US. Subcommittees include the Subcommittee on Courts, the Internet, and Intellectual Property; the Subcommittee on Immigration, Border Security, and Claims; the Subcommittee on Commercial and Administrative Law; the Subcommittee on Crime, Terrorism, and Homeland Security; and the Subcommittee on the Constitution.

House Committee on Resources

The House Committee on Resources has jurisdiction over issues pertaining to fisheries and wildlife, forest reserves and national parks, forfeiture of land grants and alien ownership, the Geological Survey, international fishing agreements, irrigation, interstate compacts related to the allocation of water for irrigation, reclamation, Native Americans, insular possessions of the US, military parks, battlefields, national cemeteries, the establishment of monuments and memorials, mineral land laws and claims, mineral resources on public land, mining interests, mining schools and laboratories, marine affairs, oceanography, petroleum conservation on public lands, preservation of prehistoric ruins, public lands, US government relations with Native Americans and Native American tribes, and the trans-Alaska oil pipeline. Subcommittees include the Subcommittee on Energy and Mineral Resources; the Subcommittee on Fisheries and Oceans; the Subcommittee on Forests and Forest Health; the Subcommittee on National Parks; and the Subcommittee on Water and Power.

House Committee on Rules

The House Committee on Rules has two subcommittees. The first subcommittee is the **Subcommittee on the Rules and Organization of the House**. This subcommittee has responsibilities concerning issues regarding the relationship between the House of Representatives and the Senate, as well as issues regarding the relationship between Congress and the Judicial Branch. The Subcommittee on the Rules and Organization of the House also has responsibilities related to the internal operations of the House of Representatives. The second subcommittee is the **Subcommittee on the Legislative and Budget Process**. This subcommittee has responsibilities concerning issues regarding the relationship between Congress and the Executive Branch. The Subcommittee on the Legislative and Budget Process also has responsibilities related to the Congressional budget process.

House Committee on Science

The House Committee on Science has jurisdiction over issues pertaining to all federal scientific research and development that is not military related. The committee has jurisdiction over the National Aeronautics and Space Administration, the Department of Energy, the Environmental Protection Agency, the National Science Foundation, the Federal Aviation Administration, the National Oceanic and Atmospheric Administration, the National Institute of Standards and Technology, the Federal Emergency Management Agency, the US Fire Administration, and the US Geological Survey. Subcommittees of the House Committee on Science include the Subcommittee on Environment, Technology, and Standards, the Subcommittee on Energy, the Subcommittee on Research, and the Subcommittee on Space and Aeronautics.

House Committee on Small Business

The House Committee on Small Business has jurisdiction over issues pertaining to the Small Business Administration, financial and management programs and technical assistance programs for small businesses, advocacy for small businesses, issues related to veterans and small businesses, technology and research assistance programs for small businesses, the Small Business Technology Transfer program, federal procurement, government competition and regulatory flexibility, paperwork reduction, government regulation, taxation, energy, the Government Performance and Results Act, empowerment for small businesses in high-risk areas, workforce issues, health care, pensions, e-commerce, telecommunications, international trade, self-employment, manufacturing, agricultural and rural matters, and review of relevant regulations. The subcommittees of the House Committee on Small Business include the Subcommittee on Workforce, Empowerment, and Government Programs; the Subcommittee on Regulatory Reform and Oversight; the Subcommittee on Tax, Finance, and Exports; and the Subcommittee on Rural Enterprises, Agriculture, and Technology.

House Committee on Standards of Official Conduct

The House Committee on Standards of Official Conduct implements the **ethics program** for the House of Representatives, as each branch of the federal government has the responsibility of implementing its own ethics program. Each house of the legislative branch has its own ethics committee to implement its ethics program; the counterpart to the House Committee on Standards of Official Conduct is the Senate Select Committee on Ethics. The House Committee on Standards of Official Conduct has jurisdiction over issues pertaining to the **House Code of Official Conduct**. The committee has jurisdiction to create or administer standards of official conduct; to investigate violations of the code of official conduct, laws, and regulations; to provide reports to government authorities of evidence of violations of laws; to give opinions about the appropriateness of the conduct of individuals associated with the House of Representatives; and to review requests for exceptions to the gift rule, and has jurisdiction over the Ethics in Government Act and the Foreign Gifts the Decorations Act.

House Committee on Transportation and Infrastructure

The House Committee on Transportation and Infrastructure has jurisdiction over issues pertaining to aviation, the Coast Guard and maritime transportation, economic development, public buildings, emergency management, highways, public transit, pipelines, railways, and water resources and environmental issues. The subcommittees of the House Committee on Transportation and Infrastructure include the Subcommittee on Aviation; the Subcommittee on the Coast Guard and Maritime Transportation; the Subcommittee on Economic Development, Public Buildings and Emergency Management; the Subcommittee on Highways, Transit, and Pipelines; the Subcommittee on Railroads; and the Subcommittee on Water Resources and Environment.

House Committee on Veterans' Affairs

The House Committee on Veterans' Affairs has jurisdiction over issues pertaining to **veterans** in a broad sense. The committee also has jurisdiction over pensions for veterans of all wars and over life insurance provided by the federal government for veterans of the armed services. In addition, the House Committee on Veterans' Affairs has jurisdiction over issues pertaining to the compensation of veterans and over vocational training and educational programs for veterans. The committee also has jurisdiction over veterans hospitals, medical services for veterans, civil relief for sailors and soldiers, services that assist individuals who have served in the armed forces in acclimating from life in the armed forces back into civilian life, and national cemeteries. The committee has specific jurisdiction over the Department of Veterans Affairs. Subcommittees include the Subcommittee on Disability Assistance and Memorial Affairs, the Subcommittee on Economic Opportunity, the Subcommittee on Health, and the Subcommittee on Oversight and Investigations.

House Committee on Ways and Means

The House Committee on Ways and Means has jurisdiction over customs, collection districts, ports, reciprocal trade agreements, broad efforts to generate revenue, efforts to generate revenue that are specifically associated with US insular possessions, US government debt, deposit of public funds, duties on goods, organizations that are exempt from paying taxes, and social security. Subcommittees of the House Committee on Ways and Means include the Subcommittee on Trade, the Subcommittee on Oversight, the Subcommittee on Health, the Subcommittee on Social Security, the Subcommittee on Human Resources, and the Subcommittee on Select Revenue Measures.

House Permanent Select Committee on Intelligence

The House Permanent Select Committee on Intelligence has the responsibility for overseeing many government organizations and their activities, including the Central Intelligence Agency, the Defense Intelligence Agency, the Department of Defense, the Department of Energy, the Department of Homeland Security, the Department of Justice, the Department of State, the Department of Treasury, the Federal Bureau of Investigation, the National Geospatial-Intelligence Agency, the National Reconnaissance Office, the National Security Agency, the Office of Naval Intelligence, the US Air Force Intelligence, Surveillance, and Reconnaissance, the US Army Intelligence and Security Command, the US Coast Guard, and the US Marine Corps Intelligence Department. Subcommittees of the House Permanent Select Committee on Intelligence include the Subcommittee on Terrorism/HUMINT, Analysis, and Counterintelligence, the Subcommittee on Technical and Tactical Intelligence, the Subcommittee on Intelligence Policy, and the Subcommittee on Oversight.

Election Process and Powers of the House of Representatives

Members of the House of Representatives are elected for **two-year terms**. Each state has at least one Representative, and the number of Representatives in each state depends upon its **population** as reported in the most recent census. Each state is divided into **congressional districts**. There is a Representative for every congressional district, who is elected by the voters in that district. There are 435 members of the House of Representatives, and Congress has the power to alter the total membership. A Representative must be at least 25 years old, a citizen of the United States for at least seven years, and a resident of the state to which they are elected. The House of Representatives has the power of impeachment.

Senate

There are 100 members of the **United States Senate**. The US Constitution stipulates that the **Vice President** of the United States controls the Senate and is therefore referred to as the president of the Senate. However, in reality, the Vice President is not regularly in attendance when the Senate is in session; rather, the Vice President is typically only in attendance during significant ceremonial events and when he is required to vote to break a tie within the Senate. The Senate is solely responsible for either confirming or disapproving of **treaties** that are drafted by the United States President. The Senate is also solely responsible for either confirming or disapproving of **appointments** made by the United States President, including Cabinet-level appointments, officers, Supreme Court judges, and ambassadors. In addition, the Senate is solely responsible for **trying government officials** who commit crimes against the United States.

Standing Committees of the Senate

Although Congressional committees are created to address changing political, social, and economic conditions, there are a number of committees that are permanent, known as **standing committees**. The standing committees within the Senate include the Agriculture, Nutrition, and Forestry Committee; the Appropriations Committee; the Armed Services Committee; the Banking Committee; the Budget Committee; the Commerce, Science, and Transportation Committee; the Energy and Natural Resources Committee; the Environment and Public Works Committee; the Finance Committee; the Foreign Relations Committee; the Governmental Affairs Committee; the Health, Education, Labor, and Pension Committee; the Indian Affairs Committee; the Judiciary Committee; the Rules and Administration Committee; the Small Business Committee; and the Veterans' Affairs Committee.

Senate Standing Committee on Agriculture, Nutrition, and Forestry

The Standing Committee on Agriculture, Nutrition, and Forestry was created in the year 1825. The committee writes legislation that addresses nutrition and food programs, the promotion of United States agricultural products in global markets, the development of rural areas, agricultural research, and conservation programs. The main legislation associated with the committee is known as the Farm Bill. Subcommittees of the Senate Standing Committee on Agriculture, Nutrition, and Forestry include the Subcommittee on Production and Price Competitiveness; the Subcommittee on Forestry, Conservation, and Rural Revitalization; and the Subcommittee on Research, Nutrition, and General Legislation.

Senate Standing Committee on Appropriations

The Senate Standing Committee on Appropriations was created in 1867. The committee is the biggest in the US Senate. It is responsible for **appropriating funds** before money from the US treasury can be spent. The committee allocates money to government agencies, departments, and organizations every year. Appropriations may not exceed the budget limits established by the Senate Budget Committee. There are twelve subcommittees of the Appropriations Committee that review the President's budget requests, listen to expert testimonies, and draft spending plans. Subcommittees pass information they gather to the Senate Appropriations Committee, which can review and change spending bills before passing them to the Senate to be considered. Subcommittees include Agriculture, Rural Development, and Related Agencies; Commerce, Justice, and Science; Defense; District of Columbia; Energy and Water; Homeland Security; Interior and Related Agencies; Labor, Health, and Human Services; Education and Related Agencies; Legislative Branch; Military Construction and Veterans Affairs; State, Foreign Operations, and Related Programs; Transportation; Treasury; the Judiciary; and Housing and Urban Development and Related Agencies.

Senate Standing Committee on Armed Services

The Senate Standing Committee on Armed Services is concerned with aeronautical and space matters associated with military operations and weapons development; defense; the Department of Defense, the Department of the Army, the Department of the Navy, and the Department of the Air Force; the Panama Canal; research and development associated with and carried out by the military; nuclear energy issues that are related to national security; naval petroleum reserves outside of Alaska; salaries and benefits for military personnel and their families; the selective service; and materials needed for defense. The committee is also responsible for investigating issues pertaining to defense policy in the US. Beneath the full committee are the Subcommittee on Airland, the Subcommittee on Emerging Threats and Capabilities, the Subcommittee on Personnel, the Subcommittee on Readiness and Management Support, the Subcommittee on Seapower, and the Subcommittee on Strategic Forces.

Senate Standing Committee on Banking, Housing, and Urban Affairs

The Senate Standing Committee on Banking, Housing, and Urban Affairs is concerned with financial institutions, price control for commodities, rents and services, deposit insurance, maintaining a stable economy and keeping up defense production, promoting exports and stimulating foreign trade, establishing export controls, federal monetary policy, financial assistance for commerce and industry, issuing and redeeming notes, money and credit, the building of nursing homes, public and private housing, renegotiation of Government contracts, urban development, and public transportation. Beneath the full committee are the Subcommittee on Securities and Investment, the Subcommittee on Financial Institutions, the Subcommittee on Housing and Transportation, the Subcommittee on Economic Policy, and the Subcommittee on International Trade and Finance.

Senate Standing Committee on Budget

The Senate Standing Committee on the Budget was created in 1974. The Senate Standing Committee on the Budget has the responsibility for writing the **annual Congressional budget plan** and also for tracking actions related to the federal budget. The jurisdiction of the Senate Standing Committee on the Budget extends to oversight of the operation of the Congressional Budget Office. The purpose of the Senate Standing Committee on the Budget preparing the budget plan, also referred to as the budget resolution, is to lay out a general map for Congress with regard to the levels of government revenues and expenditures that are possible for the entire government. However, other Congressional Committees also draft legislation, and this legislation drafted by other committees is the legislation that enacts policies related to government spending and taxing.

Senate Standing Committee on Commerce, Science, and Transportation

There have been many predecessors to the Senate Standing Committee on Commerce, Science, and Transportation. The committee as it exists and is named today was previously known simply as the Committee on Commerce; the name was changed to its current name in 1977. Along with the change in name, the scope of the committee's jurisdiction was expanded. The standing committee and its subcommittees deal with the Coast Guard, coastal zone management, communications, highway safety, inland waterways, and interstate commerce. In addition, the committee addresses marine and ocean navigation, safety, and transportation; deepwater ports; marine fisheries; merchant marine and navigation; aeronautical and space sciences that are not military in nature; oceans; weather; and atmospheric activities; the Panama Canal and other canals that connect oceans; regulation of consumer products and services; regulation of interstate transportation; science; engineering; and technology R&D and policy; sports; standards and measurement; transportation; and transportation and commerce aspects of Outer Continental Shelf lands.

Senate Standing Committee on Energy and Natural Resources

The Committee on Energy and Natural Resources is the successor of the Committee on Public Lands, a very old Congressional committee, and therefore the jurisdiction of the committee has existed for nearly two hundred years. The name was changed from the Committee on Public Lands to the **Committee on Energy and Natural Resources** in 1977. The full committee has jurisdiction over energy policy, nuclear waste policy, privatization of federal government assets, territorial policy, issues pertaining to Native Hawaiian concerns, and ad hoc matters that include those which necessitate an expedited process, those which overlap the specialties of multiple subcommittees, and those which hold national importance. The Committee on Energy and Natural Resources has several subcommittees, including the Subcommittee on Energy, the Subcommittee on National Parks, the Subcommittee on Public Lands and Forests, and the Subcommittee on Water and Power.

Senate Standing Committee on Environment and Public Works

The full Senate Standing Committee on Environment and Public Works has the responsibility for overseeing issues pertaining to biotechnology, the Council on Environmental Quality, Earth Day, the Convention on International Trade in Endangered Species, environmental conflict resolution, environmental education, environmental justice, the Environmental Protection Agency, environmental treaties, the Morris K. Udall Foundation for Scholarship and Excellence in National Environmental Policy, the National Environmental Education Act of 1969, the Noise Control Act of 1972, noise pollution, and nominations. There are a number of subcommittees of the Senate Standing Committee on Environment and Public Works, including the Subcommittee on Transportation and Infrastructure; the Subcommittee on Clean Air, Climate Change, and Nuclear Safety; the Subcommittee on Fish, Wildlife, and Water; and the Subcommittee on Superfund and Waste Management.

Senate Standing Committee on Finance

The Senate Standing Committee on Finance has jurisdiction over issues pertaining to the debts of the United States, customs, collection districts, ports, deposit of public money, general revenue sharing, health programs of the Social Security Act or funded by special taxes or trust funds, social security, reciprocal trade agreements, revenue measures, tariffs and import quotas, and transportation of goods to which a duty is applied. The Senate Standing Committee on Finance has jurisdiction over the activities of a number of federal offices. The committee consists of several subcommittees, including the Subcommittee on Health Care, the Subcommittee on International Trade, the Subcommittee on Long-term Growth and Debt Reduction, the Subcommittee on Social Security and Family Policy, and the Subcommittee on Taxation and IRS Oversight.

Senate Standing Committee on Foreign Relations

The Senate Standing Committee on Foreign Relations was created in 1816 as one of ten original Senate committees. The committee has jurisdiction over issues pertaining to acquiring property for US embassies, US boundaries, diplomatic service, foreign economic, military, technical, and humanitarian assistance, foreign loans, the Red Cross when it is operating internationally, international matters related to nuclear energy, international conferences and congresses, international law, International Monetary Fund and other international monetary organizations, international intervention and war, efforts to foster US commercial interests internationally, national security, ocean and international environmental and scientific matters, protection of US citizens abroad, international relations, treaties, the United Nations, and the World Bank and other international development assistance organizations. Subcommittees include the Subcommittee on International Economic Policy, Export, and Trade Promotion; the Subcommittee on Near Eastern and South Asian Affairs; the Subcommittee on European Affairs; the Subcommittee on East Asian and Pacific Affairs; the Subcommittee on African Affairs; the Subcommittee on Western Hemisphere, Peace Corps, and Narcotics Affairs; and the Subcommittee on International Operations and Terrorism.

Senate Standing Committee on Health, Education, Labor, and Pensions

The Senate Standing Committee on Health, Education, Labor, and Pensions has jurisdiction over issues pertaining to education, labor, health, public welfare, aging, agricultural colleges, the arts and humanities, biomedical research and development, child labor, convict labor, the Red Cross when it is operating within the US, equal employment opportunity, Gallaudet College, Howard University, Saint Elizabeth's Hospital, people with disabilities, labor standards, labor statistics, settling labor disputes, occupational safety and health, private pension plans, public health, railway labor and retirement, foreign laborers, student loans, wages, and hours of labor. Subcommittees of the Senate Standing Committee on Health, Education, Labor, and Pensions include the Subcommittee on Retirement Security and Aging, the Subcommittee on Education and Early Childhood Development, the Subcommittee on Employment and Workplace Safety, and the Subcommittee on Bioterrorism and Public Health Preparedness.

Senate Standing Committee on Homeland Security and Governmental Affairs

The Senate Standing Committee on Homeland Security and Governmental Affairs has jurisdiction over issues pertaining to the Department of Homeland Security, the national archives, budget and accounting issues, the census and collecting statistics, Congressional organization, the Federal Civil Service, government information, intergovernmental relations, the District of Columbia, nuclear export policy, organization of the executive branch of the government, the postal service, and the status of officers and employees of the government. The subcommittees of the Senate Standing Committee on Homeland Security and Governmental Affairs include the Subcommittee on Federal Financial Management, Government Information, and International Security; the Permanent Subcommittee on Investigations; and the Subcommittee on Oversight of Government Management, the Federal Workforce, and the District of Columbia.

Senate Standing Committee on Judiciary

The Senate Standing Committee on Judiciary was created in 1816 as one of ten original Senate committees. The Senate Standing Committee on Judiciary has broad jurisdiction in the Senate over many matters, including jurisdiction over the **courts**. The committee also has jurisdiction over antitrust policy and competition policy, the rights of consumers, the Constitution, civil rights, and property rights. In addition, the Senate Standing Committee on Judiciary has jurisdiction over matters pertaining to corrections and rehabilitation and matters involving criminal activities and drugs, immigration, border security, citizenship, intellectual property rights, terrorism, technology, and homeland security.

Senate Standing Committee on Rules and Administration

The Senate Standing Committee on Rules and Administration has jurisdiction over issues pertaining to the administration of the Senate Office Buildings, the Senate branch of the Capitol Building, the rules and procedures that are used to organize Congress, Senate rules and regulations, corrupt activities, qualifications for Senators, federal elections, the government printing office and the printing of the Congressional record, Congressional meetings, attendance at Congressional meetings, use of funds from the Senate contingent fund, succession to the office of President, the procurement of books and manuscripts and the establishment of monuments and memorials, the Senate Library and artifacts in the Senate Office Buildings and in the Senate branch of the Capitol, services provided to the Senate, the US Capitol and congressional office buildings, the Library of Congress, the Smithsonian, and the Botanic Gardens.

Senate Standing Committee on Small Business and Entrepreneurship

The Senate Standing Committee on Small Business and Entrepreneurship was created in 1981 as the successor to the Select Committee on Small Business. The Senate Standing Committee on Small Business and Entrepreneurship has jurisdiction over the **Small Business Administration**. The Senate Standing Committee on Small Business and Entrepreneurship also has jurisdiction over legislation that is pertaining to other issues extending beyond those addressed by the Small Business Administration but that are requested to be investigated by the Senate Standing Committee on Small Business and Entrepreneurship. The Senate Standing Committee on Small Business and Entrepreneurship Study is also responsible for investigating topics of concern to small businesses in the United States.

Senate Standing Committee on Veterans Affairs

The Senate Standing Committee on Veterans Affairs was established in 1970. The committee has jurisdiction over the compensation of veterans, the life insurance provided to veterans of the armed forces by the United States government, national cemeteries, the pensions of all wars of the United States, the acclimation of individuals who have served in the armed forces back into civilian life, civil relief for soldiers and sailors, the administration of veterans hospitals, medical care for veterans, in a broad sense all efforts made on behalf of veterans, and vocational training and educational services provided to veterans.

Senate Committee on Indian Affairs

The Senate Committee on Indian Affairs was permanently established in 1984 after years as a temporary committee. The Senate Committee on Indian Affairs has jurisdiction over investigating the matters that pertain to the **Native American**, **Native Hawaiian**, and **Alaska Native** populations in the United States. The committee also has jurisdiction to propose legislation that is aimed at relieving matters of difficulty for these populations. Some of the matters that have been addressed by the committee are education for Native American populations, economic development, land management, trust responsibilities, health care, and cases made by Native Americans against the US government.

Senate Select Committee on Ethics

The Senate Select Committee on Ethics has jurisdiction over issues pertaining to the **Senate Code of Conduct**. The committee implements the ethics program for the Senate, as each branch of the federal government has the responsibility of implementing its own ethics program. Each house of the legislative branch has its own ethics committee to implement its ethics program; the counterpart to the Senate Select Committee on Ethics is the House Committee on Standards of Official Conduct. Specifically, the Senate Select Committee on Ethics addresses issues involving the ethics and conduct of individuals associated with the Senate that are related to financial disclosure, gifts, travel reimbursements, honoraria bans, constraints on outside employment, conflicting interests, constraints on employment activities after serving the Senate, campaign activities, money for Senate-related business, mailings, employment practices, interventions with other government agencies, and annual budget limits.

Senate Select Committee on Intelligence

The Senate Select Committee on Intelligence was established to investigate and to provide oversight of **US government intelligence activities and programs**. The committee is responsible for conducting investigations and providing them to the Senate, which in turn can use the materials that were gathered in the investigations to generate legislative proposals. The committee is also responsible for providing reports to the Senate on US government intelligence activities and programs. The committee is charged with ensuring that US government agencies that are involved with intelligence activities provide information on intelligence that is required for the executive branch and the legislative branch to develop well-informed policies and to make good decisions regarding national security. The committee also has the responsibility of providing oversight of US government intelligence activities to make sure that they are consistent with and comply with the US Constitution and laws.

Senate Special Committee on Aging

The Senate Special Committee on Aging was originally a temporary committee that was created in 1961, but it became a permanent committee in 1977. Because of its status as a special committee, it does not possess legislative authority. However, it can investigate matters of pertinence, and it does have the ability to oversee relevant programs. The Senate Special Committee on Aging addresses issues that are pertinent to older Americans. The committee provides the results of its investigations to the Senate and also makes legislative recommendations to the Senate. The committee also publishes documents that address public policies that are relevant to older Americans. The committee studies issues related to Medicare, pensions, and employment for older Americans. It also works to stop fraudulent activities that are aimed at the elderly.

Election Process, Length of Term, Qualifications, and Powers of the Senate

Senators are elected for terms of **six years**. The Senate is composed of **two** Senators from each state. Every two years, one-third of the Senate is up for re-election. Senators were originally chosen by their state legislatures, but with the passing of the **17th Amendment** in 1913, Senators are now elected directly by voters within their state. A Senator must be at least 30 years old, a citizen of the United States for at least nine years, and a resident of the state to which they are elected. The Senate has the power to try all impeachments.

Oversight Powers of Congress

Congress is afforded certain **oversight powers** that enable it to exert influence over the Executive branch of the US government. Congressional oversight is significant for a number of reasons; it stops waste and fraud, upholds civil liberties and rights, makes sure that the executive branch is in compliance with the law, serves as a means of gathering data and information that is necessary to make laws and to inform the public, and provides a means for evaluating the performance of the executive branch of government. Congressional oversight is applicable to the Cabinet, to all executive agencies, to regulatory commissions, and to the President.

Types of Congressional Oversight

There are a number of ways that Congress can exercise **oversight** of the executive branch of government in order to ensure a system of **checks and balances** and to exert influence over **public policy**. Some of the mechanisms available to Congress include the use of committee hearings, discussions and meetings with the President and other executive officials, reports from the President, the power of the Senate to advise and approve nominations made and treaties drafted by the President and to hold trials for impeached officials, the power of the House to impeach, the ability of Congress to address the order of succession of the Presidency, membership in government commissions, and studies by Congressional committees and Congressional support agencies.

Authorization and Appropriations

Authorization laws create, perpetuate, or alter federal programs, and they are required by House and Senate rules or laws before Congress can appropriate funds in the federal budget for the programs. **Direct spending**, also known as mandatory spending, involves expenditures for programs that are authorized by legislation that concurrently includes budget authority for the expenditures. **Discretionary spending** involves expenditures that are set annually by Congress. Discretionary spending is optional, as opposed to mandatory funding. An authorization can be permanent until Congress changes it, or an authorization can be applicable only in particular fiscal years. When an authorization expires, Congress can reauthorize the authorization through the legislative process. If an **appropriation** is made after the associated authorization expires, it is referred to as an unauthorized appropriation.

Joint Committee on Printing

The Joint Committee on Printing has the responsibility of overseeing the activities of the **United States Government Printing Office**. In addition, the **Joint Committee on Printing** has jurisdiction and oversight over all of the printing processes and procedures that are used within the federal government. The Joint Committee on Printing must make sure that all federal government organizations and individuals who represent the federal government are acting in accordance with the laws that are relevant to printing, and it must also make sure that all government organizations and individuals representing the government comply with Government Printing and Binding Regulations.

Joint Committee on Taxation

The Joint Committee is made up of ten members. Five members are from the Senate Committee on Finance, three of which represent the majority and two which represent the minority; the remaining five members are from the House Committee on Ways and Means, and again three of these represent the majority and two represent the minority. The committee has a key role in the **legislative process** as it pertains to **taxes**. The committee investigates internal revenue taxes, investigates efforts that could be made to simplify taxes, provides reports summarizing its investigations to the House Committee on Ways and Means and the Senate Committee on Finance and makes legislative recommendations, and reviews tax refunds that exceed two million dollars. The committee is required to provide a yearly report to Congress that lists refunds that exceed two million dollars, including the names of the individuals and businesses that are associated with these refunds and the exact amounts that are refunded.

Joint Committee on the Library

The Joint Committee on the Library is responsible for overseeing issues pertaining to the **Library of Congress**. The committee consists of five members, each from both the Senate and the House of Representatives, for a total of ten members. Specifically, membership consists of the chair and four members of the Senate Committee on Rules and Administration, as well as the chair and four members of the Committee on House Administration. The seat of the chair is alternately held by a member of the House of Representatives or the Senate each time that Congress convenes. There are no subcommittees for the Joint Committee on the Library. The committee was created in 1802 for the purpose of assisting with the expansion of a congressional library. Today, in addition to overseeing the Library of Congress, the committee also has jurisdiction over the art collection of

Congress and the Botanic Garden. The committee can accept works of art on behalf of Congress and assign a spot in the US Capitol to display the art.

Joint Economic Committee

The Joint Economic Committee was established in 1946 when Congress passed the Employment Act of 1946. It was one of two advisory committees established under the **Employment Act of 1946**. The other committee established under this act was the President's Council of Economic Advisers. The purpose of both of these committees is to study and investigate economic conditions and to make recommendations regarding possible efforts to better **economic policy**. The Joint Economic Committee is chaired by either a member of the Senate or a member of the House of Representatives; each time Congress convenes, the chair alternates between the two chambers of Congress.

A Bill

A bill is a piece of legislation that is formally introduced in Congress. A bill can originate in either the House of Representatives or in the Senate. When a bill originates in the House of Representatives, it is designated as **H.R**. When a bill originates in the Senate it is designated by **S**. Bills are numbered in consecutive order. Bills can be categorized into either public bills or private bills. **Public bills** address general issues. If a public bill is both approved by Congress and signed by the President, it is passed and becomes a Public Law, or a Public Act. In contrast, **private bills** address individual circumstances. For example, private bills might be introduced to address a case against the Federal Government, immigration and naturalization cases, or land titles. If a private bill is both approved by Congress and signed by the President, it is passed and becomes a private law.

How Laws are Passed

Bills for raising **revenue**, such as those for taxes, originate in the House of Representatives. All bills must pass both the Senate and the House of Representatives in the exact same form. A bill that passes in both houses is sent to the President, who can either sign the bill or veto it. If the President **signs** the bill, it becomes law. If the President **vetoes** the bill, it is sent back to Congress, and if both the House and the Senate pass it by a two-thirds majority, the bill becomes law, thereby overriding the President's veto. If the President neither vetoes a bill nor signs it within ten days after receiving it from Congress, it becomes a law without his signature. However, if Congress sends a bill to the President and then adjourns, it does not become law if the President does not sign the bill within ten days; this is known as a **pocket veto**.

State, County, and City Government

City Government

Approximately eighty percent of the United States population resides in **urban areas** or areas immediately surrounding urban areas. Therefore, **city governments** are an integral part of the general system of government within the United States. City governments provide direct services to their citizens, even more so than the federal government or state governments. Examples of services that are provided by city governments include police forces and firefighting forces, health and sanitation, education, public transportation, and housing. City governments are chartered by state governments; the city charter outlines the objectives and powers allocated to the city. While many city governments operate independently from state governments, many large cities work in collaboration with state and federal governments. The organization of city governments varies, but the majority have a **central council** that is chosen by the people through an election, as well as an **executive officer** who is aided by department heads. Traditionally, there are mayor-council city governments, commission city governments, and city manager city governments.

County Government

A county is a subregion within a state. Counties typically consist of at least two towns and a number of villages. Usually, a single city or town within a county is named as the **county seat**. The county seat serves as the site at which government offices are situated. The county seat is also where the board of commissioners for the county convenes. Small counties have boards that are selected by the entire county. In contrast, large counties have commissioners who represent each town, city, or district within the county. **County boards** are responsible for setting county taxes, appropriating funds, setting pay rates for county personnel, overseeing county elections, building and upkeep of highways and bridges, and managing federal, state, and county social welfare programs.

Town and Village Government

Many governments are too tiny to be classified as city governments. Such small jurisdictions are known as **towns** and **villages** and receive a charter from a state. Town and village governments address only **local matters** such as maintaining local roads, illuminating local roads, managing a local water supply, maintaining local police and firefighting forces, developing and implementing local health policies, providing or organizing the disposal of waste locally, setting local taxes, and managing local schools. Town and village governments are typically overseen by a board or a council that is chosen through election. A chairperson or a president can serve as the chief executive officer of the board or council. Alternatively, an elected mayor can serve as the chief executive officer of the board or council. Town and village governments can be staffed by clerks, treasurers, police and fire officers, and health and welfare officers.

Town Meetings

Some local governments hold what are referred to as **town meetings**. Town meetings have occurred for more than two hundred years. The townships that hold town meetings are typically found throughout New England states. Town meetings are a rather unique characteristic that distinguishes some small-town governments from other forms of government. Town meetings are typically held on an annual basis, but they can be held more often if necessary. At a town meeting, registered voters assemble in an open meeting to elect officers, discuss local matters, and vote on local legislation that concerns the operation of the local government. The attendees of the town meeting make decisions together as a community concerning issues such as road maintenance, building public facilities, tax rates, and town budgets.

State versus Federal Government

Initially, government systems in the United States were characterized as **state governments** that were essentially self-governed. These circumstances in the early days of the United States represented an aversion to the **centralized government** that was present in England, the colonial power that first controlled America. The state government system proved to be insufficient, and, therefore, the **Constitution** was written to delineate the powers afforded to a **federal government**. The Constitution also delineates the relationship between the federal and state governments. The system instituted in the Constitution is known as a federalist system, in which powers are shared between the federal and state governments. Specific powers are allocated to the federal government, while other powers remain in the hands of state governments.

Concurrent Powers

While both the national and state governments reserve specific powers that the other does not have, there are certain powers that are shared between them. These shared powers are known as **concurrent powers**. The concurrent powers that are shared by both the national government and the state governments include the power to collect taxes, the power to build roads, the power to borrow money, the power to create courts, the power to create and enforce laws, the power to establish banks and corporations, the power to spend funds in the interest of the general welfare of the United States and its citizens, and the power to take private property for purposes that benefit the public so long as just compensation is provided.

State Constitutions

In the United States, state governments each have a unique **state constitution**. State constitutions resemble the federal Constitution in many ways. However, state constitutions may not be in disaccord with the federal Constitution. State governments have control over affairs that occur **within state boundaries**, such as communications within state boundaries; regulations concerning property, industry, business, and public utilities; criminal codes; and labor conditions. There are also numerous matters over which state and federal governments **share jurisdiction**. State constitutions differ from one another regarding some issues, but they are typically laid out similarly to the federal Constitution. All state constitutions contain a section on people's rights and a section that outlines how government should be organized. Every state constitution also stipulates that ultimate authority rests with the people and establishes specific standards and values as the basis of government.

State Executive and Legislative Branches

State governments are divided into executive, legislative, and judicial branches, just as in the federal government. In a state government, the **governor** serves as the head of the **executive branch**. The governor is elected by popular vote for a term of either two or four years, depending on the state. Every state in the US has a **bicameral legislature** except Nebraska, which has a single legislative body. The bicameral legislature is divided into an upper house and a lower house. The upper house is typically referred to as the **Senate**, as in the federal government, and the lower house can be referred to by a number of names, including the **House of Representatives**, the **House of Delegates**, or the **General Assembly**. State senators typically serve for a term of four years, while members of the House of Representatives, House of Delegates, or the General Assembly serve for a term of two years.

State and Local Courts

Every state has a **court system** that is independent and distinct from the federal court system. The hierarchy of the state court system includes **trial courts** at the lowest level; **appellate courts** are the highest courts in the state court system. The great majority, over ninety-five percent, of the court cases in the United States are heard and decided in state courts and local courts, which also fall under the jurisdiction of the states. Depending on the state, there may be one or two appellate courts within the state. States organize and name their courts differently. Typically, lower courts are assigned specific names and authority to hear specific types of cases, such as family courts and probate courts. Beneath the specialized trial courts are more informal trial courts, including magistrate courts and justice of the peace courts, which typically do not involve a jury.

Mayor-Council City Governments

The mayor-council form of city government has existed the longest among the types of city governments in the United States. In a city where there is a **mayor-council** form of government, there is a **mayor** who is elected by the people to serve as the chief executive officer of the city. There is also a **city council** that is elected by the people. The members of the city council represent the regions that make up the legislative branch. The mayor is responsible for appointing the people who head the numerous city departments. The mayor can also appoint other city officials. The mayor has the power to veto the laws of the city, which are also referred to as city ordinances. The mayor may also draft the budget for the city. The city council is responsible for passing the laws of the city, establishing city property taxes, and allocating funds among city departments.

Commission City Governments

The commission form of city government represents a blending of the executive and legislative duties into one assembly of city officials known as the **city commission**. There are typically three or more members of the city commission, and they are chosen in a city-wide election. Every member of the city commission is charged with overseeing the responsibilities of at least one department of the city. One member of the city commission is selected to be the chairperson of the commission. The chairperson of the city commission is sometimes referred to as the mayor of the city. However, the chairperson of the city commission does not have any power above and beyond that of the other members of the city commission.

City Manager City Governments

The city manager form of city government began in an effort to meet the needs of complicated issues that are common in modern-day American cities. Meeting this complicated mix of issues requires experience and knowledge in a variety of matters, as well as managerial skills. Traditional elected officials do not always hold such skills, knowledge, and expertise. To overcome this problem, some city governments have opted to have a single individual serve in the position of **city manager**, with the responsibility for exercising executive powers. City governments based on the city manager system have a relatively small **city council** that is chosen through election. This city council creates city ordinances and develops city policies. The city manager is hired by the city council to implement the laws and policies developed by the council. The city manager is also responsible for creating a city budget and overseeing city departments. There is typically no limit to the amount of time that an individual may serve in the position of city manager.

Separation of Powers in State and Local Governments

Government at both the federal and state levels is characterized by a **separation of powers**. At the local level, the organization of government is different. State and local government often distinguishes between **executive powers** and **law enforcement powers** by allowing citizens to choose public prosecutors through elections. In some states citizens elect judges as well. In local governments, the election of individuals who represent special authority, such as police chiefs and members of school boards, serves to separate such individuals from the executive and legislative branches of government. At the local level, juries also have a significant role in maintaining the system of checks and balances, as they have the sole authority to determine the facts in most criminal and civil cases, restricting the power of the executive and judicial branches in enforcement of laws.

POWERS OF STATE GOVERNMENTS

Each state government reserves the **power** to issue state licenses, the power to regulate business and commerce within the boundaries of the state, the power to hold elections, the power to create local governments, the power to ratify Constitutional amendments, and the power to regulate public health and safety. The state governments may also exercise powers that are not explicitly stipulated in the United States Constitution as being held by the federal government. Similarly, the state governments may exercise powers that the Constitution does not explicitly restrict the states from exercising.

POWERS OF THE FEDERAL GOVERNMENT

The national, or federal, government reserves **powers that are not afforded to the states**. The national government has the power to print money, regulate business and commerce between states and between the United States and other countries create treaties and carry out foreign policies, declare war, maintain military forces, and create post offices. The national government also has the power to create laws that are deemed essential to carrying out all of the other powers that are constitutionally granted to the national government.

POWERS DENIED TO STATE GOVERNMENTS

There are a number of powers that are denied to state governments within the United States of America. These **restrictions** are stipulated by the **Constitution** of the United States. States are restricted from doing anything that the federal government is restricted from doing. States are also restricted from forming alliances or confederations. States are restricted from declaring war and maintaining navies. State governments are restricted from making and entering into treaties with foreign countries. In addition, state governments are restricted from making money. State governments are also restricted from placing taxes on imports and exports from or to other states, respectively. States are restricted from preventing the requirements of a contract from being met as well. Finally, states are restricted from taking away an individual's rights without due process of law.

POWERS DENIED TO THE FEDERAL GOVERNMENT

There are a number of powers that are denied to the national, or federal, government of the United States of America. These **restrictions** are stipulated by the **Constitution** of the United States. The federal government is restricted from breaking or abusing the Bill of Rights. The federal government is also restricted from placing taxes on exports from one state to another state. In addition, the federal government is restricted from using funds from the United States Treasury unless an appropriations bill is passed and approved. Finally, the federal government is restricted from altering state borders.

POWERS DENIED TO BOTH THE FEDERAL GOVERNMENT AND STATE GOVERNMENTS

There are a number of powers that are denied to both the federal government and state governments in the United States of America. These **restrictions** are stipulated by the **Constitution** of the United States. The federal government and state governments are restricted from conferring titles of nobility. Both levels of government are also restricted from allowing slavery to take place; this restriction is specifically stated in the thirteenth amendment of the United States Constitution. The federal and state governments are also restricted from prohibiting citizens of the United States from exercising their right to vote based on race, color, or based on previous conditions of servitude; this restriction is specifically stated in the fifteenth amendment of the United States Constitution. Finally, both the federal and state governments are also restricted from prohibiting citizens of the United States from exercising their right to vote based on gender; this restriction is explicitly stated in the nineteenth amendment of the United States Constitution.

Appeals

If a case originates in a state court, it typically must be **appealed** within the state court system and have exhausted all possible appeal options within the state court system before it is possible to appeal the case within the federal court system. Also, in order for a case that has originated within the state court system to be appealed within the federal court system, the case must have something to do with a **federal issue**. If a decision is made by a state supreme court and the case involves a federal issue, it can be appealed to the US Supreme Court. The US Supreme Court then has the authority to overturn state laws.

Police Powers of the State Courts

State courts have the authority to exercise what are referred to as **police powers** over specific issues. These issues include health, morals, and safety. For example, in order to ensure the health of citizens, a state government can mandate that all children enrolled in school must receive vaccinations against particular diseases. If anyone wanted to challenge such a mandate issued under the police power of the state, they would have to do so in a state court. Police powers are granted by the **tenth amendment** of the United States Constitution. However, most state constitutions also include a Bill of Rights unique from the federal Bill of Rights that restricts the state's power over its citizens.

State Court Judges

State court judges may take their seats in state courts in a number of ways. State judges can be **appointed** to state courts by a state governor. After a specific period of time has elapsed, these appointed judges may run in an election. State judges can also be initially **elected** to their seat in a state court, rather than first being appointed. Elections for judgeships are sometimes contested and partisan in nature. However, sometimes elections for these positions are not contested and not partisan in nature. States often try to better state and local judges by establishing pools of qualified legal professionals for state governors to select appointees from.

State Legislatures

There are over seven thousand state legislators throughout the fifty states. Term limits exist for these legislatures in a number of states, but not all. There are also over thirty-five thousand staff members that have positions with state legislatures.

Organization and Procedures of State Legislatures

The organization and procedures of state legislatures serve as the foundation for state legislatures. Specifically, the key procedural components of state legislatures include **parliamentary procedures**; every state legislature establishes its own parliamentary procedures. Procedures also include those that are in place to effectively and efficiently operate **committees**; most legislatures have created personnel policies to organize the staff that carries out everything from research to security and from budgeting to technology support. State legislatures are organized at many levels in order to ensure that legislative staff members are working effectively and efficiently. One of the means of ensuring organization is through legislative sessions and session dates. **Legislative sessions** can be characterized as regular legislative sessions, which meet at regularly scheduled intervals, or as special or extraordinary legislative sessions, which are called by either the governor of a state or by the legislature itself with the purpose of addressing specific issues.

Tied Chambers in State Legislatures

A tied chamber occurs in a state legislature when the political parties represented in the legislature are equally divided. Usually, this is not the case. Normally, one political party has control over the state legislature. However, in recent times it has become more common for state legislative chambers to be **divided equally** along party lines. Such an equal division along party lines does not necessarily mean that there will be a political deadlock within the state legislature. There are a number of methods that state legislatures use to move forward past a stalemate, including a coin toss, a vote by the lieutenant governor, statutory laws to guide legislatures through a deadlock situation, and negotiated agreements.

Georgia Government

Georgia State Constitution

The current Georgia State Constitution is organized into eleven **Articles**. Each Article is divided into a number of sections. Each paragraph of the section is numbered, and divided into clauses designated with a lower-case letter. Before the first Article, there is a short preamble. In order, the Articles are: Bill of Rights, Voting and Elections, Legislative Branch, Constitutional Boards and Commissions, Executive Branch, Judicial Branch, Taxation and Finance, Education, Counties and Municipal Corporations, Amendments to the Constitution, and Miscellaneous Provisions. At the end, the Constitution includes a table showing the number of amendments proposed, ratified by the General Assembly, and rejected by the General Assembly by year.

Principles

The **Georgia State Constitution** is intended "to perpetuate the principles of free government, insure justice to all, preserve peace, promote the interest and happiness of the citizen and of the family, and transmit to posterity the enjoyment of liberty" (Constitution, Preamble). To meet these goals, the document lays out **regulations** governing all aspects of life in Georgia. Previous versions used difficult language that has been eliminated in the current version, which has been revised for clarity and brevity. The Bill of Rights ensures the basic rights of Georgia citizens. The Voting Article covers who may vote, election rules, and laws governing public officials. The Legislative Branch section describes the composition of the General Assembly and its duties. Constitutional Boards and Commissions describes the setup of state boards and organizations. The Executive Branch section discusses the structure of the Governor's office, the Governor's duties, and the installation and removal procedures for Executive officers. The Judicial Branch Article describes the structure of the courts, rules governing judgeships, and other legal procedures. The Taxation and Finance, Education, and Counties sections discuss specific rules regarding taxation, tax collection, education, and the way the state is divided into counties.

Rights and Responsibilities of Georgia Citizens in State Government

The rights of Georgia citizens are spelled out in the state's **Bill of Rights**. Citizens are free to pursue life, liberty, and property, and these rights are equally protected for all citizens. Religious discrimination is not permitted, and free speech and free press are protected. Citizens may bear arms and have the right to a trial by jury and legal counsel. Penalties in jail and bail amounts must be reasonable, and people may not be tried twice for the same crime unless an appeal is granted or a mistrial is declared. Involuntary servitude is outlawed. The state government is set up for the benefit of Georgia citizens, and it is their right and responsibility to regulate it and change it. Citizens have the right to vote, so that they may regulate their government and be involved in improving it.

Voting Requirements and Electoral Process in Georgia

US citizens who are at least 18 years old and reside in Georgia may **vote**, as long as they have not been convicted of a felony that they have not yet made restitution for. Citizens who are mentally incompetent may not vote. **Voter registration** can be done by mail at a number of public facilities, but must be completed by 30 days before an election. Elections must be conducted by **secret ballot**. Elections are conducted annually, and fifteen state-level offices may be elected: governor, lieutenant governor, two senators, secretary of state, attorney general, school superintendent, agriculture commissioner, labor commissioner, insurance commissioner, and five public service commissioners. The Georgia Supreme Court and the Georgia Court of Appeals are also elected. Local offices filled by election also include General Assembly representatives, county, and city officers. Other public authorities may also be elected. Current election procedure uses a touch-screen computer with three backup devices to minimize election problems.

Role of Political Parties in Georgia Government

Having at least two political parties moderates Georgia's government and provides room for philosophical debate. The first system in the state was the **Federalist Party**, opposed by the **Democratic-Republican Party**. By the 1830s, the two parties were the **States' Rights Party** and the **Union Party**. These parties merged with the **Democratic Party** and the **Whigs**, respectively. The Whig party later collapsed, and **Republicans** came to Georgia during Reconstruction. Between 1870 and 1960, Georgia was consistently Democratic. After that, Republicans gained a foothold and the two-party system was refreshed. Throughout Georgia's history, third parties have also been key in the outcome of some elections by splitting the vote of one of the main parties, which usually allows the other party to win the election. In Georgia, a **political party** is defined by law as a group that received at least 20% of the votes for governor or president in a general election. A **political body** is a group that can collect 1% of Georgia voters' signatures on a petition or in a statewide election vote. Political bodies may only place candidates on the ballot for local and statewide offices. Third parties must collect signatures equal to 5% of the number of registered voters in order to place a candidate on the ballot for district-office elections.

City Governments in Georgia

In Georgia, cities and towns operate under a **charter of municipal incorporation** approved by the state assembly, which controls their existence and boundaries. The charter describes the basic governmental structure of the city. The city government oversees anything pertaining to **public life**. This includes protecting the citizens in emergencies with fire and police responders, protecting the environment and overseeing solid and sewer sanitation, levying taxes, spending money on public works, managing public transportation and roads, and planning laws for city growth and zoning. City governments in Georgia are one of three types: the strong mayor-council, the weak mayor-council, or the council-manager. In the **strong mayor-council form**, the mayor represents the executive branch and the council represents the legislative branch. The mayor oversees the running of the government and the council adopts legislation and ordinances that dictate government policies. The **weak mayor-council form** shares the duties between the mayor and the city council. The mayor is the primary executive body, but his or her duties may also be primarily ceremonial. In the **council-manager format**, the city council decides policy and hires a manager to carry them out.

County Governments in Georgia

Currently, there are 159 **counties** in Georgia. The large number of counties reflects Georgia's rural history; nearly each town was a county seat, which gave rural residents a cultural, judicial, and political center and also enhanced their representation in state government. Counties' duties are numerous. They issue license plates and taxes, hold court, register voters, maintain roads, administer public assistance, probate wills, maintain police and fire forces, oversee garbage collection and hospitals, manage parks and recreation, govern sewage and water management, build libraries, and preserve building codes. These numerous roles provide all of Georgia's citizens with services similar to those available in cities, even if they live in rural areas.

Georgia General Assembly Members, Governor, and Lieutenant Governor

Georgia General Assembly House members must be 21 years old, have lived in their districts for a year, and in the state for at least two years. **Senate members** must be 25 years old and meet the same residency requirements. **House members** serve on committees focused on state business. The committees develop legislation that then passes to the House. The Senate has similar committees. Terms are two years. The **governor** must be at least 30 years old, a US Citizen for at least 15 years, and a Georgia resident for at least 6 years. The governor may be elected for two consecutive four-year terms, but must relinquish the position for four years before running again. The governor is the top executive and law enforcement officer, making him the commander in chief of the state's military. He can veto legislation and appoint officials to fill in gaps until the next election. He also oversees the state budget and can award discretionary money to specific projects. The **lieutenant governor** must meet the same qualifications as the governor. He may be re-elected an unlimited number of times. This office is voted separately from the governor. The lieutenant governor fills the governor's office until the next general election if the governor cannot hold office and presides over the state senate. Informal duties of this office are to appoint members to statewide committees.

Organization of Georgia General Assembly

The Georgia General Assembly is divided into two chambers, the **House of Representatives** (180 members; lower house) and the **Senate** (56 members; upper house). Each chamber is divided into committees whose party composition is the same as that of the chamber. These committees discuss and debate issues that affect the state. The leader of the House of Representatives is the **Speaker of the House**, who is a member of the majority political party and who is elected by the entire chamber. This person schedules debates, votes, and can assign representatives to committees. The majority and minority parties are also presided over by the majority and minority leader, whose functions are to advance their parties' interests. If a bill is approved by the House, it passes to the Senate. The Senate is also divided into committees which debate and introduce legislation. The **lieutenant governor** presides over the Senate instead of a Speaker. The **president pro tempore** of the Senate is the leader of the majority party. Duties of the Georgia Assembly include introducing new legislation, amending the Georgia State Constitution, passing the state budget every year, and re-drawing legislative districts every decade.

Major Policy Areas Covered by Georgia State Programs

Georgia state programs fall mainly into executive, legislative, and judicial categories. **Executive programs** include the Department of Agriculture; the Department of Labor; Insurance and Fire Safety; Public Services; and the offices of Executive members which includes the governor, lieutenant governor, attorney general, secretary of state, and the state school superintendent. These programs are all designed to protect and improve the lives of Georgia citizens. **Legislative programs** include the General Assembly, voting, lawmaking, and districting. These programs are intended to permit Georgia citizens to participate in their government. **Judicial programs** include all the courts of the state, which are in place to protect the liberties of citizens and to address any wrongdoing.

Steps Followed by a Bill That Becomes Georgia Law

Issues raised in the **Georgia House of Representatives** begin when a legislator drafts a bill or resolution. He usually relies on the **Office of Legal Counsel** to write the actual text to make sure it is in the correct format. The bill summary, or title, is read aloud on the floor of the house on three separate days. The bill is assigned to a committee for consideration. Bills that are favorably considered by their committees are forwarded to consideration by the entire House. Debates and questions follow, amendments may be suggested, and the bill is voted on. If it passes the House, it moves on to the Senate. The same process occurs, and the bill is sent back and forth between House and Senate until it is either rejected or approved upon by both bodies. If approved, the bill is then sent on to the governor for consideration. He may sign the bill within 40 days or he may veto it. His veto can be overridden by a two-thirds majority of the Senate.

Georgia Court System and Selection of Judges

The Georgia court system has limited, general, and appellate courts. **Limited-jurisdiction courts** include magistrate courts, probate courts, county courts, and juvenile courts. These courts oversee smaller legal issues, such as small civil suits, violation of county ordinances, misdemeanors, traffic violations, juvenile violations and issuing search warrants. **General-jurisdiction courts** are the superior courts of the state, and they oversee any felony and any civil or criminal case. **Appellate-jurisdiction courts** are the Court of Appeals and the Supreme Court. These courts rule on cases generated in the other two levels of the judicial system. Except for juvenile courts, judges of limited-jurisdiction courts are elected every four years in general or partisan elections by the geographic unit over which they would preside. Juvenile court judges are appointed by superior court judges in four-year terms. Part-time judges may continue to work as lawyers separately from their judicial work. General-jurisdiction, or superior court judges, are also elected for four-year terms by the public. Appellate court judges are elected for six-year terms by the public.

Juvenile and Adult Justice Systems in Georgia

The **juvenile justice system** of Georgia is applied to delinquent children under the age of 17 and deprived children under 18. In situations concerning capital felonies, custody, and parental rights, the juvenile justice system works with the superior courts. Juvenile courts oversee issues of traffic violations as well as violent felonies such as murder, rape, and armed robbery. Trials are not conducted in front of a jury, and issues go directly to the Court of Appeals or the Supreme Court if there is a problem. Designated detention centers are used for juvenile offenders, and rehabilitation is an important goal. The **adult justice system** applies to everyone over the age of 17. Trials are typically conducted in front of a jury unless the issue is addressed in magistrate court. Probate and magistrate issues may be addressed in Superior Court before they are sent to the Court of Appeals or Supreme Court. Sentencing tends to be harsher than in the juvenile system.

Chapter Quiz

Ready to see how well you retained what you just read? Scan the QR code to go directly to the chapter quiz interface for this study guide. If you're using a computer, simply visit the online resources page at **mometrix.com/resources719/gacepolsci** and click the Chapter Quizzes link.

Citizenship and Politics

United States Politics

Political Parties

A political party is an organization that advocates a particular ideology and seeks to gain power within government. The tendency of members of political parties to support their party's policies and interests relative to those of other parties is referred to as **partisanship**. Often, a political party is comprised of members whose positions, interests, and perspectives on policies vary, despite having shared interests in the general ideology of the party. As such, many political parties will have divisions within them that have differing opinions on policy. Political parties are often placed on a **political spectrum**, with one end of the spectrum representing conservative, traditional values and policies and the other end of the spectrum representing radical, progressive values and policies.

Types of Party Systems

There is a variety of party systems, including single-party systems, dominant-party systems, and dual-party systems. In a **single-party system**, only one political party may hold power. In this type of system, minor parties may be permitted, but they must accept the leadership of the dominant party. **Dominant-party systems** allow for multiple parties in opposition of one another, but the dominant party is the only party considered to have power. A **two-party system**, such as in the United States, is one in which there are two dominant political parties. In such a system, it is very difficult for any other parties to win an election. In most two-party systems, there is typically one right-wing party and one left-wing party.

Right-Wing Political Parties and Left-Wing Political Parties

Right-wing political parties in the United States of America are typically associated with conservatism or Christian democracy. **Right-wing political parties** and politics are considered to be the opposite of left-wing political parties and politics. In the United States of America, the **Republican Party** is the dominant right-wing political party. **Left-wing political parties** are typically associated with socialism, social democracy, or liberalism. In the United States of America, the **Democratic Party** is the dominant left-wing political party.

Democratic Party

The Democratic Party was founded in 1792. In the United States, it is one of the two dominant political parties, along with the Republican Party. The **Democratic Party** is to the left of the Republican Party. The Democratic Party began as a conservative party in the mid-1800s, shifting to the left during the 1900s. There are many factions within the Democratic Party in the United States. The **Democratic National Committee (DNC)** is the official organization of the Democratic Party, and it develops and promotes the party's platform and coordinates fundraising and election strategies. There are Democratic committees in every US state and most US counties. The official symbol of the Democratic Party is the **donkey**.

Republican Party

The Republican Party is often referred to as the **GOP**, which stands for Grand Old Party. The **Republican Party** is considered socially conservative and economically neoliberal relative to the Democratic Party. Like the Democratic Party, there are factions within the Republic Party that agree with the party's overall ideology but disagree with the party's positions on specific issues.

The official symbol of the Republican Party is the **elephant**. The **Republican National Committee (RNC)** is the official organization of the Republican Party, and it develops and promotes the party's platform and coordinates fundraising and election strategies. There are Republican committees in every US state and most US counties.

POLITICAL CAMPAIGNS

A political campaign is an organized attempt to influence the decisions of a particular group of people. Examples of campaigns could include elections or efforts to influence policy changes. One of the first steps in a campaign is to develop a **campaign message**. The message must then be delivered to the individuals and groups that the campaign is trying to reach and influence through a campaign plan. There are various ways for a campaign to **communicate** its message to the intended audience, including public media; paid media such as television, radio and newspaper ads, billboards, and the internet; public events such as protests and rallies; meetings with speakers; mailings; canvassing; fliers; and websites. Through these efforts, the campaign attempts to attract additional support and, ultimately, to reach the goal of the campaign.

ELEMENTS OF A CAMPAIGN

THE MONEY AND THE MACHINE

Money is a significant aspect of a campaign because with changes in technology, campaigns have become increasingly expensive to run. Some of the costs associated with running a campaign include TV advertisements, mailings, and campaign staff salaries. **Fundraising** is often used to generate money to cover campaign costs. The capital that is necessary to run a campaign refers to human capital, which may consist of paid staff, volunteers, or a combination of both. Key members of a campaign include a campaign manager, people to make strategic decisions, and people to canvass door-to-door and make phone calls.

THE CAMPAIGN MESSAGE

Political campaigns consist of three main elements, which are the campaign message, the money that is necessary to run the campaign and "machine," and the capital that is necessary run the campaign. A campaign message is a succinct statement expressing why voters should support the campaign and the individual or policy associated with that campaign. The message is one of the most significant aspects of a political campaign, and a considerable amount of time, money, and effort is invested in devising a successful campaign message, as it will be repeated throughout the campaign and will be one of the most identifying factors of the campaign.

VOTING

Voting is a method of decision-making that allows people to express their opinion or preference for a candidate or for a proposed resolution of an issue. In a democratic system, **voting** typically takes place as part of an **election**. An individual participates in the voting process by casting a vote, or a **ballot**; ballots are produced by states. A secret ballot can be used at polls to protect voters' privacy. Individuals can also vote via absentee ballot. In some states, voters can write-in a name to cast a vote for a candidate that is not on the ballot. Some states also use straight-ticket voting, allowing the voter to vote for one party for all the elected positions on the ballot.

DIFFERENT VOTING SYSTEMS

Different types of voting systems exist in the United States of America. In a **single-vote system**, the voter can only vote for one option, precluding the voter from voting for anyone else. Alternatively, in a **multiple vote system**, the voter may vote for multiple options. In a **ranked vote system**, a voter may rank alternative options in order of preference. In a **scored, or rated, vote system**, the voter gives each option a score that falls on a scale between one and whatever number represents the upper boundary of the scale.

Voter Eligibility

The United States Constitution establishes that individual people are **permitted to vote** in elections if they are citizens of the United States and are at least eighteen years old. The **fifteenth** and **nineteenth amendments** of the United States Constitution stipulate that the right to vote cannot be denied to any United States citizen based on race or sex, respectively. States regulate voter eligibility beyond the minimum qualifications stipulated by the United States Constitution. Depending on the regulations of individual states, individuals may be denied the right to vote if they are convicted criminals.

Voter Registration

Individuals have the responsibility of **registering to vote**. Every state except North Dakota requires citizens to register to vote. In an effort to increase voter turnout, Congress passed the **National Voter Registration Act** in 1993. The Act is also known as "Motor Voter," because it required states to make the voter registration process easier by providing registration services through drivers' license registration centers, as well as through disability centers, schools, libraries, and mail-in registration. Some states are exempt because they permit same-day voter registration, which enables voters to register to vote on the day of the election.

Elections in the United States

In the United States, officials are **elected** at the federal, state, and local levels. The first two articles of the Constitution, as well as various amendments, establish how **federal elections** are to be held. The President is elected **indirectly** by electors of an electoral college. Members of the electoral college nearly always vote along the lines of the popular vote of their respective states. Members of Congress are **directly** elected. At the state level, state law establishes most aspects of how elections are held. There are many elected offices at the state level, including a governor and state legislature. There are also elected offices at the local level.

Primaries and Caucuses

Candidates for federal office are chosen by primaries and caucuses. In a **primary election**, voters in a jurisdiction choose a political party's candidate for a later election. Candidates for state-level offices are also selected through primaries. The purpose of a **caucus** is also to nominate candidates for a later election. A caucus is a meeting that takes place in a precinct with the purpose of discussing each party's platform and voting issues such as voter turnout. Eleven states hold caucuses. The period of time known as the primary season in Presidential elections, which includes both primaries and caucuses, lasts from the Iowa caucus in January to the last primary, ending in early summer.

Political Media

The political media includes forms of the media that are owned and overseen and managed or influenced by political entities. The purpose of the **political media** is to disseminate the views and platforms of the associated political entity. The media is often referred to as a **fourth power**, in addition to the executive, legislative, and judicial branches of the government. The **internet** has become an additional form of political media. However, the internet is not completely identifiable as a political medium, given the lack of a central authority and the lack of a common political method of communication via the internet.

Petition

A petition is a request to an authority, most commonly a government official or public office or agency. A **petition** typically takes the form of a document that is addressed to an official who holds authority and that is signed by multiple individuals. In addition to **written petitions**, people may submit **oral petitions**, and today petitions are often internet-based. The First Amendment to the US Constitution contains a clause known as the **Petition Clause**, which guarantees the right "to petition the Government for a redress of grievances." The right to petition includes the right to file lawsuits against the government. Petitions can be used for many purposes. One example includes petitions to qualify candidates for public office to appear on a ballot; in order for a candidate's name to appear on a ballot, the candidate must collect signatures from voters. Other types of petitions include those used in efforts to generate support for various causes.

Protest

A protest is an expression of opposition to, and sometimes of support of, events or circumstances. **Protests** represent a means for individuals to publicly make their views heard in an effort to influence public opinion or government policy, or as a means to enact **change**. Protests generally result when self-expression of opposing views is restricted by government policy, political or economic circumstances, religion, social structures, or the media, and people react by declaring their views through cultural mechanisms or on the streets. There are numerous forms of protest, including boycotts, civil disobedience, demonstrations, non-violent protests, picketing, protest marches, protest songs, riots, sit-ins, teach-ins, strikes, and others.

Advantages and Disadvantages to the Two-Party System

Advocates of the two-party system argue that the advantages of such systems are that they are **stable** because they enable policies and government to change slowly rather than rapidly due to the relative lack of influence from small parties representing unconventional ideologies. In addition, they seem to drive voters towards a middle ground and are less susceptible to revolutions, coups, or civil wars. Among the critiques of the two-party system is the claim that stability in and of itself is not necessarily desirable, as it often comes at the expense of **democracy**. Critics also argue that the two-party system promotes negative political campaigns, in which candidates and their respective parties only take positions on issues that will differentiate themselves from their opponents, rather than focusing on policy issues that are of significance to citizens. Another concern is that if one of the two major parties becomes weak, a **dominant-party system** may develop.

Constitution Party

The Constitution Party is a conservative minority party in the US that was originally founded as the US Taxpayers Party in 1992; its name was changed in 1999. The **Constitution Party** represents the third-largest percentage of registered voters in the US. Members believe that US laws originate from the Bible, take a very conservative approach to social issues such as homosexuality and abortion, and push for a more prominent role of religion in the lives of US citizens. Members also support a **stricter conformity** to what they interpret as the original intent of the US Constitution and the principles of the Declaration of Independence. The Constitution Party supports limiting federal government by reducing taxes, regulations, and spending, particularly social programs such as welfare, education, and healthcare. The party is also opposed to US involvement in international affairs, illegal immigration, and governmental welfare, and interprets the Second Amendment as securing the individual right to own guns.

Green Party

The Green Party is a **liberal minority party** that has been in existence since the 1980s. However, it was not until the presidential campaigns of 1996 and 2000, when Ralph Nader ran as the presidential nominee on the **Green Party** ticket, that the party gained widespread recognition. Members of the Green Party have won elections predominantly at the local level in the United States, and typically in nonpartisan-ballot elections where candidates were not identified on the ballot as having an affiliation with a political party. The Green Party advocates decentralization of government and local autonomy. There are ten core values held by the Green Party, which are based on the four pillars of the Green Party in Europe. These are community-based economics, decentralization, ecological wisdom, feminism, grassroots democracy, non-violence, personal and global responsibility, respect for diversity, social justice, and sustainability.

Libertarian Party

The Libertarian Party is a minority party that was created in 1971 out of the belief that the two dominant parties in the US had deviated from the libertarian principles of the American founding fathers. The core value of the **Libertarian Party** is **individual liberty**. The Libertarian Party advocates for a limited government, an end to taxes, a minimally regulated free-market economy, the right to keep and bear arms, drug legalization, abolishment of the government social welfare system, civil liberties, a foreign policy of free trade and non-intervention, and the right to abortion. The party opposes the use of military force to achieve goals, as well as any form of gun control.

Reform Party of the United States of America

The Reform Party of the United States of America is a minority party that was founded in 1995 by Ross Perot out of the belief that US citizens were disillusioned with politics and wanted an **alternative** to the two dominant parties. Some of the issues that formed the platform of the **Reform Party** were financial reform issues, including the federal deficit and national debt; government reform issues such as term limits, campaign finance reform, and lobbying reform; and trade issues. The Reform Party advocates maintaining a balanced budget, campaign finance reform, responsible immigration enforcement, opposition to free trade agreements like NAFTA, withdrawal from the WTO, limiting social welfare programs, and term limits for US Representatives and Senators.

Modern Election Campaigns in the United States

Political campaigns in the US have changed and continue to change as advances in technology permit varied campaign methods. Campaigns represent a **civic practice**, and today they are a high-profit industry. The US has an abundance of **professional political consultants** that employ highly sophisticated campaign management strategies and tools. The election process varies widely between the federal, state, and local levels. Campaigns are typically controlled by individual candidates rather than by the parties that they are associated with. Larger campaigns utilize a vast array of media to reach their targeted audiences, while smaller campaigns are typically limited to direct contact with voters, direct mailings, and other forms of low-cost advertising to reach their audiences. In addition to fundraising and spending done by individual candidates, party committees and political action committees also raise money and spend it in ways that will advance the cause of the particular campaign they are associated with.

Canvassing

Canvassing is a method used to solicit votes from people that enables a political campaign to speak with a large number of individuals. The goals of **canvassing** efforts are to try to convince voters to vote for a candidate, to increase recognition of a candidate's name, and to generate supporters.

Canvassing can take one of two forms: field canvassing and phone canvassing. **Field canvassing** is done door to door, approaching every residence in a voting district. This method typically enables canvassers to speak with an increased number of people, who are generally more inclined to speak with someone in person than over the phone, and also enables canvassers to distribute literature and put up lawn signs. Sometimes, the candidate will also conduct field canvassing efforts. **Phone canvassing** is typically done using a phone bank, and therefore can reach even more people than field canvassing efforts. Phone canvassing is particularly useful in rural areas. However, many individuals are not receptive to unsolicited phone calls, which they associate with telemarketing.

Political Campaign Staff

The staff employed by a political campaign receive a salary in exchange for their efforts to devise and implement a strategy for a successful campaign. Campaigns are typically led by a **campaign manager**. Beneath the campaign manager are **department directors**. The various departments in a political campaign can include the field department, the communications department, the finance department, the compliance and legal departments, the technology department, and the scheduling and advance department, which sends people to events in advance of a candidate to ensure that the details of the event are in order. Beneath the department level, campaign structure varies widely. On larger campaigns, there may be multiple **coordinators**, each serving a particular function within individual departments. **Interns** and **volunteers** represent the bottom tier of the campaign, and they perform the necessary but tedious tasks of the campaign.

Presidential Elections

The President of the United States is elected **indirectly** by members of an **electoral college**. Members of the electoral college nearly always vote along the lines of the popular vote of their respective states. The winner of a presidential election is the candidate with at least 270 **Electoral College votes**. It is possible for a candidate to win the electoral vote and lose the popular vote. Incumbent Presidents and challengers typically prefer a balanced ticket, where the President and Vice President are elected together and generally balance one another with regard to geography, ideology, or experience working in government. The nominated Vice Presidential candidate is referred to as the President's **running mate**.

Electoral College

Electoral college votes are cast by state by a group of electors; each elector casts one **electoral college vote**. State law regulates how states cast their electoral college votes. In all states except Maine and Nebraska, the candidate winning the most votes receives all of the state's electoral college votes. In Maine and Nebraska, two electoral votes are awarded based on the winner of the statewide election, and the rest go to the highest vote-winner in each of the state's congressional districts. Critics of the electoral college argue that it is undemocratic because the President is elected **indirectly** as opposed to directly, and that it creates inequality between voters in different states because candidates focus attention on voters in swing states who could influence election results. Critics argue that the electoral college provides more representation for voters in small states than large states, where more voters are represented by a single electoral than in small states, and discriminates against candidates that do not have support concentrated in a given state.

Congressional Elections

Congressional elections are every two years. Members of the **House of Representatives** are elected for a two-year term, and elections occur every two years on the first Tuesday after November 1st in even years. A Representative is elected from each of 435 House districts in the US. House elections usually occur in the same year as Presidential elections. Members of the **Senate** are elected to six-year terms; one-third of the Senate is elected every two years. Per the

Seventeenth Amendment to the Constitution, which was passed in 1913, Senators are elected by the electorate of states. The country is divided into Congressional districts, and critics argue that this division eliminates voter choice, sometimes creating areas in which Congressional races are uncontested. Every ten years, **redistricting** of Congressional districts occurs. However, redistricting is often partisan and therefore reduces the number of competitive districts. The division of voting districts resulting in an unfair advantage to one party in elections is known as **gerrymandering**. Gerrymandering has been criticized as being undemocratic.

State and Local Elections

State elections are regulated by state laws and constitutions. In keeping with the ideal of separation of powers, the legislature and the executive are elected separately at the **state** level, as they are at the federal level. In each state, a governor and a lieutenant governor are elected. In some states, the Governor and Lieutenant Governor are elected on a joint ticket, while in other states, they are elected separately from one another. In some states, executive positions such as Attorney General and Secretary of State are also elected offices. All members of state legislatures are elected, including state senators and state representatives. Depending on the state, members of the state supreme court and other members of the state judiciary may be chosen in elections. **Local government** can include the governments of counties and cities. At this level, nearly all government offices are filled through an election process. Elected local offices may include sheriffs, county school boards, and city mayors.

Campaign Finance

Hard vs. Soft Money

Running a campaign requires money; however, the means of funding campaigns is often controversial. Both individuals and organizations donate significant private contributions to campaigns. Money donated to campaigns can be characterized as either hard money or soft money. **Hard money** is contributed directly to a campaign. **Soft money** is not contributed directly to a campaign and is not legally coordinated by the official campaign itself; it is, however, spent to fund efforts that benefit the candidate, such as advertising. The administration and enforcement of campaign finance law is the responsibility of the Federal Election Commission, which was created in 1975.

Disclosure

Campaign finance law mandates that candidate committees, party committees, and PACs must file reports **disclosing** the money that they fundraise and spend. Federal candidate committees must disclose all PACs and party committees that donate money to them; the names, occupations, employers, and addresses of all individuals who donate more than $200 in an election cycle; and all expenditures greater than $200 per election cycle for services rendered by an individual or vendor. States and local candidates are also mandated to disclose donations from PACs and party committees. It is becoming commonplace for campaign finance statements to be filed electronically.

Independent Expenditures

An individual or group is legally permitted to make unlimited **independent expenditures** in association with federal elections. An independent expenditure is an expenditure that is made to pay for a form of **communication** that supports the election or defeat of a candidate; the expenditure must be made independently from the candidate's own campaign. To be considered independent, the communication may not be made with the cooperation or consultation with, or at the request or suggestion of, any candidate, any committees or political party associated with the candidate, or any agent that acts on behalf of the candidate. There are no restrictions on the amount that anyone may spend on an independent expenditure; however, any individual making an independent expenditure must report it and disclose the source of the funds they used.

Activities of Political Parties

Political parties participate in federal elections at the local, state, and national levels. Most party committees must register with the **Federal Election Committee** and file reports disclosing federal campaign activities. While party committees may contribute funds directly to federal candidates, the amounts that they contribute are restricted by the campaign finance contribution limits. National and state party committees are permitted to make additional coordinated expenditures, within limits, to assist their nominees in general elections. However, national party committees are not permitted to make unlimited independent expenditures to support or oppose federal candidates using **soft money**. State and local party committees are also not permitted to use soft money for the purpose of supporting or opposing federal candidates, but they are allowed to spend soft money, up to a limit of $10,000 per source, on voter registration and on efforts aimed at increasing voter participation. All party committees are required to **register** themselves and **file disclosure reports** with the Federal Election Committee once their federal election activities exceed specified monetary limits.

Campaign Finance Reform

Reform Through the Federal Election Campaign Act

In 1974, Congress passed the Federal Election Campaign Act, requiring candidates to disclose sources of campaign contributions and expenditures. The act was amended to **limit campaign contributions**. The act limited individual contributions to $1,000 per campaign, banned direct contributions from corporations and trade unions, and limited contributions from **political action committees**, known as **PACs**, to $5,000 per campaign. A PAC is a private group that is organized on behalf of a special interest to aid in efforts to elect or defeat political candidates; the overriding goal of a PAC is to support candidates who would further legislation that is in the interest of the special interest. The number of PACs in the US exceeds 4,000 due to the increase in the creation of PACs in response to the ban on campaign contributions from corporations and trade unions. The **Federal Election Campaign Act** introduced public funding for Presidential primaries and elections and called for the creation of the **Federal Election Committee**, which administers campaign finance law.

Reform Through the Bipartisan Reform Act

In 2002, Congress passed the Bipartisan Campaign Reform Act. The act made it illegal for local and national parties to spend soft money and for national party committees to accept or spend soft money, it increased the limit placed on individual campaign contributions from $1,000 to $2,000, it banned corporations or trade unions from contributing to issue advertising directly, and it made it illegal for corporations or trade unions to fund advertisements that mention a federal candidate within 60 days of a general election or within 30 days of a primary.

Front Loading and Invisible Primaries

Sometimes, too many primaries take place early in the primary season, resulting in a reduction in the number of realistic Presidential candidates because campaign donors withdraw their support for those candidates that are not viewed as viable options; this is called **front loading**. The candidates that are most successful in their run for office are not always the candidates who do well in the early primaries. Some candidates attempt to generate support, funding, and media coverage prior to the start of the official primaries in what is referred to as the **invisible primaries**.

Public Opinion

Public opinion represents the collective attitudes of individual members of the adult population in the United States of America. There are many varied forces that may influence **public opinion**. These forces include public relations efforts on the part of political campaigns and political parties. Another force affecting political opinion is the political media and the mass media. Public opinion is very important during elections, particularly Presidential elections, as it is an indicator of how candidates are perceived by the public and of how well candidates are doing during their election campaigns. Public opinion is often measured and evaluated using **survey sampling**.

Mass Media and Public Opinion

The mass media is critical in developing **public opinion**. In the short term, people generally evaluate information they receive relative to their own beliefs; in the long term, the media may have a considerable impact on people's beliefs. Due to the impact of the media on an individual's beliefs, some experts consider the effects of the media on an individual's independence and autonomy to be negative. Others view the impact of the media on individuals as a positive one, because the media provides information that expands worldviews and enriches life, and fosters the development of opinions that are informed by many sources of information. A critical aspect of the relationship between the media and public opinion is who is in control of the knowledge and information that is disseminated through the media. Whoever controls the media can propagate their own agenda. The extent to which an individual interprets and evaluates information received through the media can influence behaviors such as voting patterns or consumer behavior, as well as social attitudes.

Survey Sampling

Survey sampling is a method that involves the random selection of a sample from a population that is fixed in size. Survey sampling is often used to measure public opinion. The simplest method of **survey sampling** is referred to as **simple random sampling**. Simple random sampling makes sure that each and every possible subset of the defined population which has the desired sample size is given the same probability of being selected. Another method of survey sampling is **stratified sampling**. In addition, **cluster sampling** and **multistage sampling** represent other methods of survey sampling.

Special Interest Groups

A special interest group is a political organization that is created to influence policy or legislators involved in a particular policy area. **Special interest groups** could include corporations, trade associations, trade unions, senior citizens or individuals with disabilities, or even groups within the legislature or bureaucracy. The goal of special interest groups is to attempt to influence government. There are two types of special interest groups: protective groups and promotional groups. **Protective groups** represent one part of society, such as professional organizations, veterans' organizations, and trade unions. Membership in protective groups is limited to individuals who are members of the organizations representing the specific part of society they do. In contrast, **promotional groups** advocate a greater cause and claim to represent the common interests of humankind. Examples of promotional groups include Greenpeace and Friends of the Earth. Membership in promotional groups is open to all individuals, and, as such, are much larger than protective groups.

United States Political Ideologies

Liberalism

Liberalism is an ideology based on the **autonomy** of individuals. **Liberalism** favors civil and political liberties and seeks to maximize those liberties under law and ensure protection from arbitrary authority. A system characterized by liberalism would possess a pluralistic liberal democratic system of government, a rule of law, the free exchange of ideas, and economic competition. The basic **principles of liberalism** include transparency; individual and civil rights, particularly the right to life, liberty, and property, equal rights for all citizens under law; and government by the consent of the governed, which is guaranteed through elections. Liberalism also favors laissez-faire economics, the free market, and the gold standard.

Libertarianism

Libertarianism is an ideology that seeks to maximize **individual rights**, **private property rights**, and **free-market capitalism**. Individuals who subscribe to the ideology of **libertarianism** believe that people should have the freedom to do what they will with their bodies and their private property as long as they do not coerce others to do the same. They also believe that individuals should have the liberty to make their own moral choices, as long as they do not use coercion to prevent others from exercising the same liberty, and that government should not prevent an individual from making a moral choice or impose moral obligations on people. Libertarians advocate minimum government involvement except to protect liberty and prevent coercion. In addition, libertarians support capitalism, oppose social welfare, and oppose government spending and programming that is not aimed at protecting liberty.

American Liberalism

American liberalism is a political ideology that is derived from classical liberalism. Like classical liberalism, **American liberalism** is defined by the ideal of **individual liberty**. However, American liberalism typically rejects laissez-faire economics and instead advocates for the creation and maintenance of institutions that foster **social and economic equity**. American liberalism began in the beginning of the 20th century and started to decline in the 1970s. American liberalism features support for government social programs, increased funding for public education, labor unions, regulation of business, civil rights, voting rights, reproductive rights, strong environmental regulations, public transportation, minimum wage requirements, government funding to alternative energy research, animal rights, gun control, and a progressive tax system. People who subscribe to American liberalism oppose the death penalty.

Nationalism

Nationalism is an ideology based upon the ideal that **identification with a nation, ethnicity, or nationality** is an essential and defining part of human social existence. **Nationalism** is thus a universal ideology. However, nationalism also refers to the ideology that one national identity is superior to others and to the view that nations benefit from acting independently rather than collectively. This view of nationalism often spawns nationalist movements, which make political claims on behalf of particular nations. Nationalists differentiate between nations based on specific criteria and also differentiate between individual people based on which nation they are a member of. The criteria used to define national identity include ethnicity, a common language, a common culture, and common values. Nationalism has had an extremely significant impact on world history and geopolitics since the **nation-state** has become the prevailing form of state. Most people in the world currently live in states which are nation-states.

Review Video: American Nationalism
Visit mometrix.com/academy and enter code: 865693

Review Video: Historical Nationalism
Visit mometrix.com/academy and enter code: 510185

CONSERVATISM

Conservatism is a political ideology that is founded on **traditional values**, a **distrust of government,** and **resistance to changes** in the established social order. Most **conservative** political parties are right-wing, but some countries do have conservative political parties that are left-wing. All conservatives place a high value on tradition, which refers to standards and institutions that have been demonstrated to foster good. Conservatives view traditional values as authoritative and judge the world by the standards they have come to believe in, including a belief in God. Conservatives consider tradition to be above the political process. They also disagree with the laws and constitutions of liberal democracies that allow behavior that is in opposition to traditional values. Conservatives in a democracy opt to participate, separate, or resist. Participation on the part of conservatives in a democracy usually takes the form of liberal republican politics, in which conservatives use government policy to promote their values. The imposition of conservative values on the public is typical of nationalist or religious conservatives.

GREEN POLITICS

Green politics is a political ideology based on **environmentalism** and **sustainability**. It is seen as an alternative to both left- and right-wing views, and individuals identifying themselves with the left or right tend to view **green politics** as distinct from their own ideology. As a movement, green politics typically grows at a slow rate but does not readily lose support to other views or parties over time. Some of the features of green politics include support of consensus decision making, participatory democracy, and deliberative democracy; green taxes; alternative measures of economic growth; opposition to the subsidy of pollution by government; opposition to nuclear power, persistent organic pollutants, and biological forms of pollution; investing in human capital; accounting reform; an end to the War on Drugs in the United States and Europe; an end to the War on Terrorism; and the curtailment of civil rights.

PACIFISM

Pacifism is an ideology that is based on **opposition to war**. **Pacifism** varies from a preference for the use of non-military means in resolving disputes to complete opposition to the use of violence or force in any situation. Pacifism may be based on principle or pragmatism. Pacifism based on principle is founded on the belief that war, violence, force, and coercion are morally wrong. Pacifism based on pragmatism is founded on the belief that there are more preferable means of resolving disputes than war, and that the costs of war outweigh the benefits. An individual who opposes war is often referred to as a **dove** or as being dovish, alluding to the peaceful nature of the dove.

REPUBLICANISM

Republicanism is a political ideology founded on the concept of a nation being governed by an **elected representative** rather than a monarch. Today, the elected representative is most often referred to as the President. A **republic** is a state in which sovereignty resides with the people, as well as a political system in which individual liberty is protected through the power of citizens to elect representatives. These representatives are responsible to the citizens who elected them, and govern according to law. **Republicanism** also represents the ideologies of the political parties that identify themselves as the Republican Party.

FEMINISM

Feminism is an ideology founded on the belief that there should be **social, political, and economic equality** between the sexes. This belief has manifested itself in a social movement known as the **feminist movement**, which advocates equal rights for women. As such, feminism typically focuses on issues that pertain to women, such as reproductive rights, domestic violence, maternity leave, equal pay, sexual harassment, sexual discrimination, and sexual violence, as well as on the themes of patriarchy, stereotyping, objectification, and oppression. In the 1960s and '70s, feminism focused on issues faced by Western, white, middle-class women while claiming to represent all women. Feminism has since progressed to focus on the connection between gender and sexuality with other social factors, such as race and class. Modern feminism addresses issues that cross class, racial, cultural, and religious boundaries, as well as issues that are specific and pertinent to individual cultures. Feminism also addresses whether particular issues associated with women, such as rape, incest, and mothering, are universal issues.

Chapter Quiz

Ready to see how well you retained what you just read? Scan the QR code to go directly to the chapter quiz interface for this study guide. If you're using a computer, simply visit the online resources page at **mometrix.com/resources719/gacepolsci** and click the Chapter Quizzes link.

United States Constitution

Presidential Succession Act of 1947

The Presidential Succession Act of 1947 established that if both the President and the Vice President are unable to execute the powers and perform the duties of the Presidency, the position will be assumed by the **Speaker of the House**, followed by the **President pro tempore of the Senate**, and then the **Cabinet members** in the following order: Secretary of State, Secretary of the Treasury, Secretary of Defense, Attorney General, Secretary of the Interior, Secretary of Agriculture, Secretary of Commerce, Secretary of Labor, Secretary of Health and Human Services, Secretary of Housing and Urban Development, Secretary of Transportation, Secretary of Energy, Secretary of Education, Secretary of Veterans Affairs, and Secretary of Homeland Security.

Marbury v. Madison

Marbury v. Madison was an 1803 Supreme Court case that established a standard for the constitutional power of the Supreme Court to carry out **judicial review of Federal statutes**. The Supreme Court decided that it had the power to invalidate a statute that it found to be in violation of the Constitution. The case set the judicial branch as an equal counterpart to the other two branches of the United States federal government. Specifically, Marbury v. Madison was the inaugural case during which the United States Supreme Court used the power of judicial review.

Review Video: Marbury v. Madison
Visit mometrix.com/academy and enter code: 573964

Judicial Review

Courts possess the power of **judicial review**, which entails reviewing laws or official actions made on the part of government representatives to determine if those laws or actions are in violation of the Constitution. In the United States, the power of judicial review is held by courts. Specifically, the **United States Supreme Court** holds the highest power to make decisions regarding the constitutionality of both state and federal laws. The doctrine of judicial review was founded based on the decision of the Supreme Court in the case of Marbury v. Madison in 1803. In states, the power of judicial review lies with the highest appellate court, which can be referred to as a **Supreme Court** or the **Court of Appeals**.

Bill of Rights

Creation of the Bill of Rights

The Bill of Rights includes the first ten amendments to the Constitution. These amendments were proposed to the states by the first Congress of the United States of America as a means to protect personal and civil liberties. The **Bill of Rights** was originally composed of twelve amendments, which were proposed by Congress on September 25, 1789. In 1791, the group of ten amendments that comprise what is known as the Bill of Rights was ratified by the states. These amendments became part of the Constitution of the United States.

Amendments 1-5

The **First Amendment** protects the five most important civil liberties of citizens of the United States. These civil liberties include the freedom of religion, the freedom of speech, the freedom of the press, the right of assembly, and the freedom to petition. The **Second Amendment** protects the right to bear arms. The **Third Amendment** protects the right of citizens not to have troops placed in their private homes. The **Fourth Amendment** protects citizens against search and seizure of their private homes without a warrant. The **Fifth Amendment** pertains to the rights of an accused person and protects the right to a trial, the right not to be tried twice for the same crime (double jeopardy), and the right against self-incrimination. The Fifth Amendment also protects the right of citizens against the taking of their private property without just compensation.

Amendments 6-10

The **Sixth Amendment**, like the Fifth Amendment, pertains to the rights of an accused person and protects the right to a speedy trial. The **Seventh Amendment** protects the right to a jury trial in civil cases. The **Eighth Amendment** places limitations on bail fines and protects against cruel and unusual punishment. The **Ninth Amendment** protects the rights of citizens that are not specifically identified in the Constitution and states that such rights shall be respected by the federal government. The **Tenth Amendment** states that certain powers are retained by the states and by the people.

Reconstruction Amendments

The Thirteenth, Fourteenth, and Fifteenth Amendments are known as the **Reconstruction Amendments**. They are grouped in this manner because they were passed during the Reconstruction period following the Civil War. They were drafted with the purpose of abolishing slavery, preventing slavery under other names, and extending rights to all citizens of the United States, regardless of race or color. Specifically, the **Thirteenth Amendment**, which was ratified in 1865, abolished slavery in the United States. The **Fourteenth Amendment**, which was ratified in 1868, established limitations on states such that no state may deny any citizen equal protection under the laws. The **Fifteenth Amendment**, which was ratified in 1870, established the right of citizens to vote regardless of race or color.

Nineteenth Amendment

The Nineteenth Amendment gave **women the right to vote**. This amendment was proposed on June 4, 1919, and was ratified on August 18, 1920. An amendment to give women the right to vote was first introduced in Congress in 1878, but it failed to pass. For the next four decades, the amendment was reintroduced in every session of Congress but was defeated each time. The involvement of women in the war effort during World War I spawned increased support for women's suffrage. Finally, in 1918, the House of Representatives approved the amendment to grant women suffrage, but the Senate defeated it. In 1919, the Senate also passed the amendment and sent it to the states for approval, where it was ratified in 1920.

Twenty-fifth Amendment

If the Presidency is vacated, the **Vice President** becomes President. If the Vice Presidency is vacated, the President **nominates** a Vice President, who must be approved by a majority vote in Congress. If the President informs Congress that he is unable to execute the powers and duties of the Presidency, the Vice President assumes the Presidency until the President informs Congress that he is able to return to office. Similarly, the Vice President will assume the Presidency if the Vice President and a majority of the Cabinet inform Congress that the President is unable to serve as President, and the President may resume office if he informs Congress that he is able to do so. The Vice President and the Cabinet can counter the President's assertion that he is able to resume office, and by a two-thirds vote within Congress, the Vice President will continue to act as President.

Review Video: Bill of Rights
Visit mometrix.com/academy and enter code: 585149

Articles of Confederation

The very first constitution in the history of the United States was the **Articles of Confederation**. The Articles of Confederation served as a plan for the government of the United States and was created on the principles that were defended during the Revolutionary War. However, the Articles of Confederation contained weaknesses. Specifically, the Articles of Confederation did not assign the power to create and collect taxes, did not assign power to oversee trade, and created a relatively weak executive power without the ability to enforce legislation. The greatest fault of the Articles of Confederation was that it did not originate with the people, but rather power was vested in the **states** to avoid a central government authority. Under the Articles of Confederation, every state could collect its own taxes, issue currency, and maintain its own militia, creating inefficiencies in the national government. The national government was primarily responsible for foreign policy and treaties. The Articles of Confederation provides learning opportunities and was a stepping stone in creating the Constitution.

Review Video: Articles of Confederation
Visit mometrix.com/academy and enter code: 927401

Governing Principles of the Constitution

The governing principles of the United States Constitution include the principle of **popular sovereignty**, which is associated with a system of government that is created by the people, for the people. Other governing principles of the United States Constitution include the rule of law, the Supreme Court, judicial review, the separation of powers, and the system of checks and balances. In addition, the governing principle of **federalism** guided the formulation of the United States Constitution, allowing for the sharing of power between the federal government and the states. The governing principles of the Constitution also included individual rights, which are embodied in the **Bill of Rights**.

Documents that Influenced the Writing of the Constitution

There are a number of documents that influenced the writing of the United States Constitution. The **Mayflower Compact** was influential; it was written in 1620 by the first settlers in the New England colony. The **Virginia Declaration of Rights** was written in 1776 and served as a prototype for other state constitutions and for the Bill of Rights. The **Declaration of Independence** was also adopted in 1776 and was influential in the writing of the Constitution. The **Articles of Confederation** was adopted in 1781 and served as the first constitution for the original thirteen states following the American Revolution. The **Federalist Papers** also served as an influence for the drafters of the US Constitution; they were published in newspapers to encourage ratification of the Constitution, which was ratified in 1788.

Review Video: Drafting the Constitution
Visit mometrix.com/academy and enter code: 662451

International Influences on the Development of the US Constitution

The US Constitution was written with the influence of **international sources and factors**. While a number of the concepts represented in the US Constitution were unique, others were taken from classical political theories and from the British model of mixed government. Specifically, the US Constitution was influenced by sections of the **Magna Carta**, which was written in the year 1215. Another influential document in the drafting of the US Constitution included the **English Bill of Rights**, which was established in 1689. Specifically, as in the English Bill of Rights, the US

Constitution mandates a trial by jury, includes the right to bear arms, and bans the application of extreme bail amounts and cruel and unusual punishments.

US Constitution

The US Constitution represents the highest law within the United States. It was the successor of the Articles of Confederation and was finished in 1787, adopted by the Constitutional Convention in Philadelphia, and subsequently ratified by the thirteen original states. The **US Constitution** established a federal union of sovereign states as well as a federal government to oversee the union. The US Constitution went into effect in 1789 and has been a model for constitutions created within other nations. The Fourteenth Amendment of the Constitution provides all United States citizens with **equal protection** under the Constitution. The judiciary branch of the federal government has the power to review the constitutionality of laws passed in the United States and can strike down laws if they are determined to be **unconstitutional**. The Fifth Article of the Constitution addresses how Congress may propose Constitutional **amendments**. In addition, a convention consisting of at least two-thirds of the states can propose Constitutional amendments. Amendments must be ratified before they become part of the Constitution.

Process of Making Amendments to the US Constitution

The process for making amendments to the US Constitution is outlined in **Article Five** of the Constitution. **Amendments** can be proposed by either two-thirds of both chambers of the United States Congress or by a convention of at least two-thirds of the legislatures of the states. Before an amendment can be included in the Constitution, it must be **ratified** by three-fourths of the legislatures of the states, or by three-fourths of special conventions that have been assembled in each of the states for the purpose of ratifying the Constitutional amendment. The President of the United States plays no official part in the process of making constitutional amendments. To date, twenty-seven amendments have been ratified and included in the Constitution.

Constitutional Interpretation

Originalism

The term *originalism* encompasses a set of theories regarding **constitutional interpretation**. People who are proponents of **originalism** believe that the meaning of the Constitution does not evolve, but is fixed and should be followed and upheld by Judges. Originalism as a form of constitutional interpretation is often favored by individuals who associate themselves with conservative political ideals in the United States. There are numerous theories that fall under the category of originalism. These theories include **original intent**, which is the opinion that Constitutional interpretation should agree with the originally intended meaning of the people who wrote and ratified the Constitution. A second theory is **original understanding**, which represents the view that people interpreting the Constitution should seek evidence of what the people who drafted the Constitution understood the Constitution to mean. The third and most followed originalist theory is **original meaning**, which is the opinion that interpretation of the Constitution should be founded on what the meaning of the words would have been at the time the Constitution was ratified.

Strict Constructionism

Strict constructionism is a form of judicial interpretation restricting judicial interpretation to the **literal meaning** of the words and phrases found in laws. **Strict constructionism** does not allow for other sources to be used or for assumptions to be made about the meaning of the laws beyond the literal words and phrases. Individuals who are proponents of strict constructionism only read text that is explicitly pertinent, and do not permit legislative intent or metaphysical ideas to influence their interpretation. People who support strict constructionism believe that if a legislative body desires to enact a law, its members are knowledgeable about how to draft it and pass it in the words that express their exact intent and meaning and that, therefore, the judiciary should not be responsible for reconstructing what the intent of the legislative body was.

JUDICIAL ACTIVISM

Judicial activism is a form of constitutional interpretation in which judicial decisions do not adhere to **precedent** or extend beyond the **limits of conventional law**. In reality, any ruling which does not fall within the limits of conventional expectations could be construed as an example of **judicial activism**. Judges are sometimes accused of judicial activism regardless of their political affiliations and views and regardless of their philosophies regarding judicial interpretation. Critics of judicial activism are concerned that judges who make decisions based on their personal beliefs are not interpreting laws on sound principles. In the US, the accusation of judicial activism often carries a negative connotation and refers to decisions that are made to further the interests of specific social or political goals. Specific acts that are associated with judicial activism in the US include the declaration that a law is unconstitutional when it is not; supporting a law that is unconstitutional; overturning judicial precedent; and ruling against the words or intent of laws or the Constitution.

LIVING CONSTITUTION

The term *Living Constitution* is often used to describe the capacity of Congress or of the states to make **amendments** to the United States Constitution. Specifically, it refers to the process of how amendments can be made that is stated in Article Five of the Constitution. The term *Living Constitution* is also often applied to characterize how the interpretation of a number of sections within the Constitution has evolved with the application of the Constitution to real-world cases throughout the history of the United States since the Constitution was adopted.

TEXTUALISM

The theory of textualism is a form of **constitutional and statutory interpretation**. Specifically, proponents of **textualism** argue that the literal meaning of the Constitution or of a statute should guide the interpretation of the Constitution or of the statute. Individuals who support textualism do not believe that non-textual resources should be used to interpret the Constitution or statutes, such as the legislative intent that was meant when the law was passed, the issue that the law was meant to address or fix, or the important questions of the judge and impartiality of the law.

PRUDENTIALISM

There exist three prudential standing principles, which means that they were judicially created. Congress can override **prudential standing principles** by passing a statute. The three prudential standing principles are Prohibition of Third-Party Standing, Prohibition of Generalized Grievances, and the Zone of Interest Test. **Prohibition of Third-Party Standing** requires that individuals can only declare their own rights and cannot declare the rights of a third party not before a court. **Prohibition of Generalized Grievances** requires that a plaintiff cannot sue if an injury is broadly shared in a similar way with a large number of individuals. The **Zone of Interest Test** is divided into two tests that are applied by the US Supreme Court. The first is the Zone of Injury, in which the nature of the injury is such that Congress expected would be covered by the statute. The second is the Zone of Interests, in which the individual is within the zone of interest covered by the statute or by the Constitution.

CONSTITUTIONAL STANDING REQUIREMENTS

The three constitutional standing requirements are injury, causation, and redressability. A plaintiff in a case must have suffered an **injury**, which is defined as an offense against a legally protected interest. An injury is required to be actual, imminent, distinct, and palpable, not abstract. There must also exist a **causal** connection between the injury and the action that the plaintiff is complaining about. Finally, it has to be highly probable and not simply speculative that a decision in favor of the plaintiff will **redress** the injury caused to the plaintiff. Congress does not have the power to alter the three **constitutional standing requirements**.

Chapter Quiz

Ready to see how well you retained what you just read? Scan the QR code to go directly to the chapter quiz interface for this study guide. If you're using a computer, simply visit the online resources page at **mometrix.com/resources719/gacepolsci** and click the Chapter Quizzes link.

Civil Rights, Civil Liberties, and Criminal Justice

Marbury v. Madison

Right before President **John Adams** left office after **Thomas Jefferson** won the presidency in the election of 1800, he passed the **Judiciary Act of 1801**. This act eliminated one seat on the Supreme Court, eliminated circuit duties for members of the Supreme Court, and created 16 federal circuit court judgeships. This allowed President John Adams to pack the federal court system with his fellow Federalists before Thomas Jefferson, a Democratic-Republican, took office. **William Marbury** was one of these individuals promised a position by John Adams. However, Adams's Secretary of State, **John Marshall**, did not have time to deliver Marbury's commission (which was the formal job offer for Marbury's position as Justice of the Peace for D.C.) before the Jefferson administration took over. The new Secretary of State, **James Madison**, refused to deliver Marbury's commission after he took office. This led to Marbury suing Madison for his commission, and the issue was brought before the Supreme Court in the case of ***Marbury v. Madison*** (1803).

Although Section XIII of the Judiciary Act of 1789 had a **Writ of Mandamus** which required Madison to honor the appointment, Chief Justice **John Marshall**, whom Adams appointed to the Supreme Court before leaving office, declared this section unconstitutional. This historic act established the doctrine of **judicial review**, which allows the Supreme Court to declare a legislative or executive act unconstitutional. Marshall thereby established an independent judiciary; he is quoted as saying, "The Constitution is the supreme Law of the Land, with the Supreme Court as the final interpreter."

McCulloch v. Maryland

When Congress chartered a national bank, the **Second Bank of the United States**, Maryland voted to tax any bank business dealing with banks chartered outside the state, including the federally chartered bank. Andrew McCulloch, an employee of the Second Bank of the US in Baltimore, refused to pay this tax. The resulting lawsuit from the State of Maryland went to the Supreme Court for judgment.

John Marshall, Chief Justice of the Supreme Court, stated that Congress was within its rights to charter a national bank. In addition, the State of Maryland did not have the power to levy a tax on the federal bank or on the federal government in general. In cases where state and federal government collided, precedent was set for the **federal government** to prevail.

The Civil Rights Act of 1871

The Civil Rights Act of 1871 was a statute passed following the Civil War. It was comprised of the **1870 Force Act** and the **1871 Ku Klux Klan Act**, and was passed primarily with the intention of protecting Southern black people from the Ku Klux Klan. Since it was passed in 1871, the statute has only undergone small changes. It has, however, been interpreted widely by the courts. In 1882, some parts of the Civil Rights Act of 1871 were found unconstitutional, but the Force Act and the Klan Act continued to be applied in civil rights cases in subsequent years.

Plessy v. Ferguson

Plessy v. Ferguson was an 1896 Supreme Court case. The case resulted in the decision that **de jure racial segregation** in **public facilities** was legal in the United States, and permitted states to restrict black people from using public facilities. The case originated when, in 1890, a black man named Homer Plessy decided to challenge a Louisiana law that segregated black and white people on trains by sitting in the white section of a train. Plessy was convicted of breaking the law in a Louisiana court, and the case was appealed to the US Supreme Court, where the Supreme Court upheld the Louisiana decision. The case established the legality of the doctrine of separate but equal, thereby allowing racial segregation. The decision was later overturned by **Brown v. the Board of Education of Topeka**.

The Fair Employment Act

The Fair Employment Act was signed by President Franklin Roosevelt in 1941. The purpose of the act was to **ban racial discrimination** in industries related to **national defense**, and it represented the very first federal law to ban discrimination in employment. The **Fair Employment Act** mandated that all federal government agencies and departments concerned with national defense, as well as private defense contractors, guaranteed that professional training would be conducted without discrimination based on race, creed, color, or national origin. The Fair Employment Act was followed by **Title VII of the 1964 Civil Rights Act**, which banned discrimination by private employers, and by **Executive Order 11246** in 1965, which concerned federal contractors and subcontractors.

Brown v. Board of Education

Brown versus the Board of Education of Topeka was a Supreme Court case that was decided in 1954. The case made it illegal for **racial segregation** to exist within **public education facilities**. This decision was based on the finding that separate but equal public educational facilities would not provide black and white students with the same standard of facilities. The case originated in 1951, when a lawsuit was filed by Topeka parents, who were recruited by the NAACP, against the Board of Education of the City of Topeka, Kansas in a US district court. The parents, one of whom was named Oliver Brown, wanted the Topeka Board of Education to eliminate racial segregation. The district court agreed that segregation had negative effects, but did not force the schools to desegregate because it found that black and white school facilities in the District were generally equal in standards. The case was appealed to the Supreme Court, where the finding was that separate educational facilities are unequal.

Bolling v. Sharpe

Bolling v. Sharpe was a 1954 Supreme Court case. Like Brown v. Board of Education, this case addressed issues concerning **segregation in public schools**. The case originated in 1949, when parents from Anacostia, an area in Washington, DC, petitioned the Board of Education of the District of Columbia to allow all races to attend a new school. The request was denied. A lawsuit was brought before the District Court for the District of Columbia on behalf of a student named Bolling and other students to admit them to the all-white school. The case was dismissed by the district court and taken to the Supreme Court. The Supreme Court ruled that the school had to be desegregated based on the Fifth Amendment.

Civil Rights Act of 1964

The Civil Rights Act of 1964 was passed to protect the rights of both **black men** and **women**. It served as part of the foundation for the women's rights movement. The act was a catalyst for change in the United States, as it made it illegal to engage in acts of **discrimination** in public facilities, in government, and in employment. The Civil Rights Act prohibited unequal voter registration, prohibited discrimination in all public facilities involved in interstate commerce, supported desegregating public schools, ensured equal protection for black people in federally funded programs, and banned employment discrimination.

The Pregnancy Discrimination Act

The Pregnancy Discrimination Act was passed in 1978 as an amendment to the sex discrimination clause of the Civil Rights Act of 1964. The **Pregnancy Discrimination Act** stipulated that people cannot be discriminated against due to pregnancy, childbirth, or medical issues related to pregnancy or childbirth. If a person becomes pregnant, gives birth, or has related medical conditions, they must receive treatment that is equivalent to that received by other employees and also receive equal benefits as other employees. The **Family and Medical Leave Act** was passed in 1993 to advance protections under the Pregnancy Discrimination Act.

Civil Rights Act of 1968

The Civil Rights Act of 1968 was passed following the passing of the Civil Rights Act of 1964. The act made it illegal to **discriminate** against individuals during the sale, rental, or financing of **housing**. Therefore, the act is also referred to as the **Fair Housing Act of 1968**. The act made it illegal to refuse to sell or rent housing based on race, color, religion, or national origin. It also made it illegal to advertise housing for sale or rent and to specify a preference to rent or sell the property to an individual of a particular race, color, religion, or national origin. In addition, the act ensured protection for civil rights workers.

Age Discrimination in Employment Act

The Age Discrimination in Employment Act of 1967 made it illegal for employers to discriminate against people who are **forty years old** or greater in age. The act establishes standards for employer-provided pensions and benefits, and mandates that information regarding the needs of older workers be made publicly available. In addition to generally banning age discrimination, the **ADEA** specifies particular actions that are illegal. Employers may not specify that individuals of a certain age are preferred or are conversely restricted from applying to job ads. Age limits are only permitted to be mentioned in job ads if age has been shown to be a bona fide occupational qualification. The act stipulates that it is illegal to discriminate against age through apprenticeship programs and that it is illegal to restrict benefits to older employees. However, employers are permitted to lower the benefits provided to older employees based on age if the expense of providing fewer or lesser benefits is equivalent to the expense of providing benefits to younger employees.

Loving v. Virginia

Loving v. Virginia was a 1967 Supreme Court case that ruled that a particular law in Virginia known as the **Racial Integrity Act of 1924** was unconstitutional, as the law had prohibited interracial marriage. The Supreme Court ruling would put an end to **race-based restrictions on marriage**. The case originated when Mildred Jeter and Richard Loving, an interracial Virginia couple that was married in Washington, DC due to the Virginia state law prohibiting interracial marriage, returned to Virginia and received charges of violating the interracial marriage ban. After pleading guilty, the couple was forced to move to DC to avoid a jail sentence, where they brought their case to the Supreme Court on the premise that their Fourteenth Amendment rights had been violated. The Supreme Court found that the Virginia law was unconstitutional and overturned the conviction that the couple had been charged with.

Jones v. Mayer

Jones v. Mayer was a 1968 Supreme Court case that ruled that Congress has the authority to **regulate the sale of private property** for the purpose of preventing racial discrimination. This United States Supreme Court ruling was based on a legal statute that stipulates that it is illegal in the United States to commit acts of racial discrimination, both privately and publicly when selling or renting property. The United States Supreme Court ruled that the congressional power to uphold the statute extends from the power of Congress to uphold the Thirteenth Amendment.

Roe v. Wade

Roe v. Wade was a controversial 1973 US Supreme Court case. The case originated in 1970 in Texas, which had an **anti-abortion law**. The plaintiff was an unmarried pregnant woman who was assigned the name "Jane Roe" to protect her identity. Texas anti-abortion law characterized the acts of having or attempting to perform an abortion as crimes, with the exception of cases in which an abortion could save the life of a mother. The lawsuit argued that the Texas law was unconstitutionally vague and was not consistent with the rights guaranteed by the First, Fourth, Fifth, Ninth, and Fourteenth Amendments. While the Texas court ruled in favor of Roe, it did not rule that Texas had to discontinue the enforcement of its anti-abortion law. Roe appealed to the Supreme Court in 1971, and the court's decision in 1973 struck down Texas's abortion laws. The case overturned most state laws prohibiting abortion. In 2022, the supreme court reversed its decision in Roe v Wade, finding no constitutional basis for requiring states to permit abortion, effectively returning the authority to the states to decide.

Regents of the University of California v. Bakke

Regents of the University of California v. Bakke was a 1978 Supreme Court case that banned **quota systems** in the college admissions process but ruled that programs providing **advantages to minorities** are constitutionally sound. The case originated when Allan Bakke, a white male who was a strong student, applied to the University of California at Davis Medical School and was rejected. The school had a program that reserved admissions spots for minority applicants; the program had grown along with the overall size of the school since its opening in 1968. Bakke complained to the school but was still not admitted, and he finally brought his case before the Superior Court of California. The California court ruled in favor of Bakke, who claimed that he had been discriminated against because of his race, and the school appealed to the US Supreme Court. The Supreme Court ruled that race could be used as one factor by discriminatory boards such as college admissions boards; however, quotas were ruled to be **discriminatory**.

Americans with Disabilities Act (ADA)

The ADA was passed by Congress in 1990. This act outlines the rights of individuals with disabilities in society in all ways besides education. It states that they should receive **nondiscriminatory treatment** in jobs, **access** to businesses and other stores, and other services. Due to this law all businesses must be wheelchair accessible, having a ramp that fits the standards of the law, and all doors and bathrooms within those businesses must be able to be used and maneuvered through by someone in a wheelchair. If these rules are not followed, businesses can be subject to large fines until these modifications have been complied with. The ADA also ensures fair treatment when applying for jobs to make sure that there is no unfair discrimination for any person with a disability who is applying to the job.

The Civil Rights Act of 1991

The Civil Rights Act of 1991 is a statute that was passed as a result of a number of Supreme Court decisions that restricted the rights of individuals who had sued their employers on the basis of discrimination. The passing of the **Civil Rights Act of 1991** was the first time since the Civil Rights Act of 1964 was passed that modifications were made to the rights granted under federal laws to individuals in cases involving **employment discrimination**. Specifically, the Civil Rights Act of 1991 granted the right to a trial by jury to individuals involved in cases of employment discrimination, and it also addressed for the first time the potential for emotional distress damages and limited the amount awarded by a jury in such cases.

Planned Parenthood v. Casey

Planned Parenthood of Southeastern Pennsylvania v. Casey was a 1992 Supreme Court case that challenged the constitutionality of Pennsylvania abortion laws. The case was brought before the US District Court for the Eastern District of Pennsylvania by abortion clinics and physicians to challenge four clauses of the **Pennsylvania Abortion Control Act of 1982** as unconstitutional under Roe v. Wade. The district court ruled that all of the clauses of the Pennsylvania act were unconstitutional. The case was then appealed to the Third Circuit Court of Appeals, which ruled to uphold all of the clauses except for one requiring notification of a husband prior to abortion. The case was then appealed to the Supreme Court, which ruled to uphold the constitutional right to have an abortion, thereby upholding Roe v. Wade.

Adarand Constructors, Inc. v. Peña

Adarand Constructors, Inc. v. Peña was a 1995 United States Supreme Court case in which the court ruled that any **racial classifications** that are instituted by representatives of federal, state, or local governments have to be reviewed and analyzed by a court. The court that reviews such racial classifications must abide by a policy of **strict scrutiny**. Strict scrutiny represents the highest standard of Supreme Court review. Racial classifications are deemed constitutional solely under circumstances in which they are being used as specific measures to advance critical and important governmental interests. The ruling of the Supreme Court in this case requiring strict scrutiny as a standard of review for racial classifications overturned the case of **Metro Broadcasting, Inc. v. FCC**, in which the Supreme Court established a two-level method of reviewing and analyzing racial classifications.

The Employment Non-Discrimination Act (ENDA) and the Equality Act

The Employment Non-Discrimination Act was a proposed United States federal law that was introduced various times before Congress but was never passed by both the House and the Senate. The **Employment Non-Discrimination Act** would ban employers from discriminating against their employees based on their **sexual orientation**. A number of states have already passed laws that ban discrimination based on sexual orientation, including California, Connecticut, Hawaii, Maryland, Massachusetts, Minnesota, Nevada, New Hampshire, New Jersey, New Mexico, New York, Rhode Island, Vermont, and Wisconsin. The ENDA has largely been encompassed by a broader resolution known as the Equality Act, which is a bill that would amend the Civil Rights Act of 1964 to further add gender identity and sexual orientation to the list of prohibited categories of discrimination for employment, public accomodations, the jury system, and housing. It has been met with opposition and has not yet been passed by both bodies of Congress.

Miranda v. Arizona

In 1966, the Supreme Court ruled that law enforcement must warn a person of their constitutional rights before interrogating them. If these rights—known as Miranda rights—are not explained to a person, that person's statements cannot be used as evidence against them at trial. The Supreme Court held that interrogating people without informing of them of their rights is in violation of their Constitutional rights.

In this case, Ernesto Miranda was arrested and charged with the kidnapping and rape of an 18-year-old woman. Miranda was not informed of his right to an attorney or to silence before or during the two-hour long interrogation he was subjected to by the police. The interrogation resulted in both oral and written confessions, which were both brought against Miranda in trial. They were initially accepted as evidence, resulting in Miranda being sentenced for 20-30 years in prison. The conviction was reversed after the Supreme Court's decision, though Miranda was later found guilty of the same crime in a later trial.

Grutter v. Bollinger

Grutter v. Bollinger was a 2003 Supreme Court case that upheld an **affirmative action policy** of the University of Michigan Law School admissions process. The case originated in 1996 when Barbara Grutter, a white in-state resident with a strong academic record, applied to the law school and was denied admission. In 1997, she filed a lawsuit claiming that her rejection was based on racial discrimination and violated her Fourteenth Amendment rights, as well as Title VI of the Civil Rights Act of 1964. The case was heard in 2001 in a US District Court, which ruled that the university's admissions policies were unconstitutional. In 2002, the case was appealed to the Sixth Circuit Court of Appeals, which overturned the lower court's decision. The case was then appealed to the US Supreme Court in 2003, which ruled that the school's affirmative action policy could remain in place, upholding the case of Regents of the University of California v. Bakke permitting race to be a factor in admissions but banning quotas.

Chapter Quiz

Ready to see how well you retained what you just read? Scan the QR code to go directly to the chapter quiz interface for this study guide. If you're using a computer, simply visit the online resources page at **mometrix.com/resources719/gacepolsci** and click the Chapter Quizzes link.

Comparitive Politics and International Relations

Study of Comparative Politics

In a **unitary government**, power is centralized. There are subdivisions or departments of the unitary government that are responsible for carrying out laws, but these bodies do not draft or pass legislation. Small countries with an ethnically and culturally homogenous population are more likely to have a unitary government. A **federal government**, on the other hand, is broken down into subdivisions, usually called states or provinces. These subdivisions are given some legal jurisdiction, though the central government usually has final authority. A large country with a diverse population is likely to have a federal government. Finally, a **confederation** is a collection of states that, while all sending representatives to a central government, do not grant the central government much power. Confederations are prone to disintegration.

Ways in Which Governments May Be Organized

Comparativists, or those who study **comparative politics**, place the political events of the present in a **historical context**. In general, these academics are concerned with creating overarching political theories that can be applied to all sorts of situations. To this end, they focus on governmental structure and its effects on the behavior of a nation and its citizenry. Comparative political scientists are especially concerned with the development and evolution of nations over time.

Parliamentary vs. Proportional Representation Forms of Government

The officials in a parliamentary government are not elected; instead, they are **selected** by their party. Candidates for **parliament** are put forth by various political parties and elected by the people. The leader of the majority party in a parliamentary system is called the **prime minister**. The prime minister takes other members of parliament to serve as his or her **cabinet**, or advisory council. One interesting feature of the parliamentary system is that elections are not held at regular intervals but are instead called by the prime minister at his or her discretion. On the other hand, in a **proportional representation** system, the electorate casts ballots for a particular **party** rather than for an **individual candidate**. Each party is given a number of seats in the legislature proportionate to its share of the vote. When there is no dominant or majority party, disparate parties must join together to create a coalition government.

Normative vs. Empirical Questions Asked by Comparativists

Comparativists must grapple with normative questions, which deal with the ethical value of political actions, and empirical questions, which concern matters of fact. In some sense, a **normative question** can only be answered with an opinion. For this reason, many political scientists eschew this sort of question. For example, comparative political scientists may avoid questions related to the morality of certain systems of government or certain political actions. Comparative political scientists are more likely to attend to **empirical questions**, which can be settled through investigation. For instance, a political scientist might try to determine the effects of different geographies or political structures on the development of a nation because many aspects of these topics can be explored through research and statistical analysis.

States, Nations, Regimes, Governments, Politics, and Political Science

- **State**: any country that has an established border, a fixed population, and its own organized government
- **Nation**: a state whose citizens share a language, a culture, and—often—a religion
- **Regime**: a particular iteration of government in a nation, usually headed by a charismatic leader. For example, Iraqis suffered for many years during the Saddam Hussein regime.
- **Government**: an organized institution responsible for making and enforcing laws in a particular area and for a particular people
- **Politics**: the set of behaviors and activities that relate to the operation of government
- **Political science**: the academic discipline concerned with the structure and operation of government

Purpose and Organization of Government

Originally, governments were created to **protect citizens and their property**. Although government systems have evolved a great deal since these origins, the basic intent is the same. There are governments representing all types of human groups. Even the smallest tribe has some sort of **organization and leadership structure**. In most cases, a national government is predicated upon a populace with a shared language and culture as well as a large and powerful middle class. This is not always the case, however, as evidenced by Canada, which has English and French Canadian as its official languages. There are several different organizational structures for governments, including communism, socialism, theocracy, confederation, hereditary monarchy, constitutional monarchy, democracy, and tribal council.

Comparative Politics

Differences in Scope and Method of Study

Comparativist political scientists are usually affiliated with one of three main approaches: rational choice comparativism, structuralism, or culturalism. A **rational choice comparativist** uses mathematics and statistics to explore politics and government. The work of a rational choice comparativist is similar to that of an economist. A **structuralist**, on the other hand, looks for similarities in political behavior in different contexts, with the aim of constructing broad, overarching theories. A structuralist seeks to advance theories that can be applied to many different nations. Finally, a **culturalist** emphasizes the details on the ground. These academics visit and often live among the people they are studying. They amass a great deal of data, which they are often reticent to apply outside of the specific context in which it was obtained.

Cultural Approach to Research

Culturalists pay particular attention to the political and cultural orientation of villages and small groups. They view **culture** as a lens through which to view **politics**. The only theories produced by culturalists are those having to do with the particular group being studied. During the 1980s and '90s, academia moved away from the culturalist approach, favoring instead the pseudo-mathematical precision of the structuralists. Another reason for the decline of the culturalist approach is the expense associated with long research trips; governments and universities have become less willing to fund these sorts of ventures.

Structural and Rational Choice Approaches to Research

As much as possible, structuralists try to rely on data gathered in the field; however, some of this data can be difficult to trust. **Rational choice political scientists**, on the other hand, rely almost exclusively on mathematics, statistics, and game theory. These academics are also interested in universally applicable theories, but they rely solely on **data** and exclude anecdotal information.

Theory of Decisions

In comparative government, the **theory of decisions** is the idea that personal political choices are influenced both by the beliefs and experiences of the decision maker and by the information provided to him. To some extent, the actors in a political system are dependent on the quality of information they receive. However, the members of a polity are likely to make vastly different decisions based on the same information. Comparative political scientists try to isolate those personal and environmental factors that exercise significant influence on political decisions.

Inference

An inference is a conclusion based on an established set of information. While an **inference** is not itself a fact, it should be based on facts. A **deductive inference** proceeds from general statements to a specific conclusion. The following is a classic example of deductive reasoning: "All men are mortal. Socrates is a man. Therefore, Socrates is mortal." **Inductive reasoning**, by contrast, proceeds from specific examples to general ideas. The following is an example of inductive reasoning: "Socrates is a man. Socrates is mortal. Therefore, all men are mortal." In political science, and especially in comparative political research, inferences are needed to make conclusions about political behavior. Some comparative political scientists focus on granular, on-the-ground research, which they use to create general theories. Other comparativists create general theories in the opposite direction by moving from general principles to specific applications.

Ideas of Dependency Theory

According to dependency theory, financial and natural resources naturally shift from **poorly developed countries** to **industrialized countries**. In other words, this theory asserts that rich states will tend to become richer, and poor states will tend to become poorer. Before this theory was advanced, many political scientists had believed that all states have a tendency toward industrialization and that the differences between states are simply due to varying degrees of progress along this path. However, dependency theory suggests that underdeveloped countries may never become developed if they are not given special assistance. Indeed, those who support this theory assert that today's underdeveloped countries are relatively less developed than any of today's industrialized countries ever were. Wealthy countries exploit the cheap labor and resources of underdeveloped nations, thereby perpetuating underdevelopment.

Policy Challenges Faced by Governments

Governments strive to meet the needs and desires of the people, but they are often restrained by **cost**. Of course, there are often disagreements between rival factions over the proper course of legislation. To pay for necessary services, a government may need to raise **taxes**, which will not be appreciated by the public. In the modern world, governments are mainly preoccupied with issues like the environment, health care, infrastructure, the economy, education, and foreign relations.

Constitution of the Federal Republic of Nigeria

In 1999, the Nigerian government affirmed a new constitution without submitting it for public approval. The **Nigerian constitution** is largely based on that of the United States: It divides the government into **legislative, judicial, and executive branches**, and it establishes **two legislative houses**. It also enumerates the fundamental **rights of Nigerians**. The Nigerian constitution asserts that political parties must be national and must have their headquarters in the capital city of Abuja. To win the presidency, a candidate must receive a majority of the total votes and at least one-quarter of the votes in two-thirds of the states. The point of these restrictions is to avoid domination by one ethnic group, though one of the practical results is to encourage two-party politics. An odd omission in the constitution was highlighted in 2009, when President Alhaji Umaru Yar'Adua fell ill. The constitution had no protocol for succession, so Vice President Goodluck

Jonathan did not have any authority when he took over. The legislature had to be assembled in a hurry to issue a special act allowing Jonathan to govern.

Constitution of Mexico

When devising their constitution, Mexico's legislators were concerned about the possibility of a single ruler dominating the country for decades. For this reason, they forbade the president from serving more than one six-year term. Also, Mexican politicians are forbidden from seeking reelection to the same office. Despite these provisions in the constitution, Mexico was dominated by the **PRI party** for years. Mexican presidents exploited the system for their own gain. The **Mexican constitution**, which was drafted on February 5, 1917, arranges the government in much the same way as that of the United States. **Article 123** outlines workers' rights including the eight-hour workday, the right to strike, and a mandatory day of rest. Until this provision was ratified, Mexico had been the scene of rampant worker exploitation. As of 2005, capital punishment was outlawed in Mexico.

Constitution of the Post-Communist Russian Federation

In 1993, Boris Yeltsin led the effort to draft and pass a constitution of the **Russian Federation**. This constitution established a government with a **strong executive branch,** somewhat limited by a legislature and a judiciary, as well as a system of checks and balances. However, whenever a national emergency was claimed, the president was allowed to seize control, dissolving the legislature and, if he desired, initiating national referenda or elections. It quickly became clear that even though this government was ostensibly ruled by the legislature, the executive could maneuver his way to a preeminent position rather easily.

Great Britain's Lack of a Written Constitution

Great Britain is an interesting model of a nation that remains stable despite **not having a formal constitution**. Britain does depend on King John's **Magna Carta of 1215** and the **Act of Settlement of 1701** (which describes the line of royal succession), but national affairs are governed in large part by case law and historical precedent. If a majority of both houses of Parliament approve, the "constitution" can be amended. This process is only complete, however, when the queen gives her royal assent. In general, the British system is founded on the supremacy of Parliament and the rule of law. In other words, **Parliament** is affirmed as the primary legislative body in the nation with the authority to determine the royal succession, control royal authority, and mandate term limits for its members.

Types of Regimes

- **Regime**: a type of government, or the duration of a particular government or leader's control in a country.
- **Authoritarian regime**: organizational structure in which one person or a small group controls the political, educational, financial, economic, and diplomatic functions of the country.
- **Totalitarian regime**: a regime that is organized around a central idea. Perhaps the best example of a totalitarian regime is the National Socialist state that existed in Germany between 1936 and 1945. Adolf Hitler and the other leaders of this movement promoted the idea that Germans were a master race engaged in a battle to the death with other ethnic groups. In the Soviet Union, leaders like Lenin and Stalin based a totalitarian regime around the idea of class struggle. In a totalitarian regime, government control is pervasive, and it is difficult for citizens to obtain or disseminate information contrary to the interests of the regime.

- **Democratic regime**: a system in which citizens have the ability to vote directly on the issues or to elect leaders. Some of the varieties of democracy include presidential, parliamentary, and veto player.

Authoritarian Regime of Joseph Stalin in the Soviet Union

Vladimir Ilyich Lenin founded the communist **Soviet Union** and was succeeded by **Joseph Stalin**. Stalin's **totalitarian** regime aimed to industrialize the country, in part by forcing the migration of peasants to the cities. Stalin stopped at nothing in pursuit of his plan. He murdered thousands of farmers who resisted forced migration, and his program for turning over the countryside to collectives resulted in massive famines that killed millions. Stalin's so-called "Five-Year Plans" established unrealistic goals for industrial production and then imposed harsh living conditions on citizens in pursuit of these goals. Stalin died in 1953, with the blood of perhaps 20 million people on his hands. Stalin's successor, Nikita Khrushchev, repudiated him in 1956.

Regime of Mikhail Gorbachev in Russia

In 1985, Mikhail Gorbachev became general secretary of the Communist Party in the Soviet Union. **Gorbachev** had three goals: **perestroika**, or industrial reform; **democratization**; and **glasnost**, or openness to the rest of the world. None of these initiatives was wholly successful. His campaign for industrial reform was stymied by production managers who did not want to take responsibility. Meanwhile, his democratization efforts resulted in the election of candidates who were not members of the Communist Party. For instance, Boris Yeltsin, not a member of the Communist Party, was elected president in 1991. Finally, the glasnost policy foundered because members of the news media were not allowed to criticize current leaders or policies, though they were permitted to criticize the leaders and policies of the past. Ultimately, Gorbachev was forced to resign, and on December 25, 1991, after surviving an attempted coup, he broke up the Union of Soviet Socialist Republics (USSR).

Regime of Boris Yeltsin in Russia

After the resignation of Gorbachev and the disbanding of the USSR, **Boris Yeltsin** took over as president of the Russian Federation. The **constitution** he delivered in 1993 placed a great deal of power with the executive, but it was approved by Russian voters. Some members of the **Duma** from the communist era conspired to overthrow Yeltsin, but he put down this nascent rebellion. Rather than gradually introduce a market economy, Yeltsin attempted "shock therapy," which caused **hyperinflation** at rates higher than 100 percent. Meanwhile, Moscow and St. Petersburg were overtaken by criminal gangs. In 1995, Russians elected very conservative and communist candidates, and in 1996, Yeltsin won reelection only because he was supported by a coalition of wealthy businessmen. His second term was marked by illness and miscalculations, leading to the crash of the ruble in 1998 and Yeltsin's ultimate **resignation** on December 31, 1999.

Regime of Vladimir Putin in Russia

Yeltsin was replaced by his final prime minister, a former KGB official named **Vladimir Putin**. Putin would prove to be a strong leader, evidenced early on by his military invasion of Chechnya after a separatist group from that region was blamed for the bombing of a Moscow apartment building in 1999. This invasion played well with the Russian populace, and after the **Unity Party**, which backed Putin, dominated the elections of December 1999, Putin himself was elected president the following March. He was able to improve the Russian economy, but the **Chechen War** dragged on, and crime became a major problem in the cities. In the 2003 elections, control of the Duma was seized by the **United Russia party**, which supported Putin. At this point, Putin's rule became more autocratic; he took control of the media and intimidated many would-be challengers to his presidency. He won reelection in a rout in 2004. The Russian constitution forbade Putin from running again in 2008, but his handpicked successor, **Dmitry Medvedev**, won the election and immediately installed Putin as prime minister, where he continues to exercise a major influence.

Totalitarian Regime of Mao Zedong in the People's Republic of China

In 1949, Mao Zedong began his twenty-seven-year reign as self-styled paramount leader. His major goal was to **industrialize** China, which at that time was a largely agrarian society. The **Great Leap Forward,** initiated in 1958, was an ambitious fifteen-year plan for modernization. It was a disaster, marked by crop shortages and starvation, and it was ultimately discontinued after only two years. Another communist program, the **Cultural Revolution**, lasted from 1966 to 1976. This was an attempt to ingrain communist values and eliminate any subversion. Youths, known as the **Red Guard**, were encouraged to turn in those they suspected of disloyalty. Those unlucky enough to be detained for subversion were beaten, sent to work camps for "reorientation," and often killed. At the same time, the Red Guard was tasked with destroying all the artifacts of pre-communist China, including buildings, artworks, and historic texts.

Authoritarian Regime of Deng Xiaoping in China

In 1976, Mao Zedong died, creating a power vacuum. After a struggle, **Deng Xiaoping** wrested control from Mao's widow, leader of the so-called "Gang of Four." After assuming the mantle of paramount leader, Deng initiated a program that loosely translates as "socialism with Chinese characteristics." This program focused on four areas of **modernization**: business, farming, education, and the military. Deng created special economic zones for foreign investment in large Chinese cities. At the same time, Deng's "mass line" approach motivated peasants to sell their surplus crops, and citizens were forbidden from having more than one child. One of the final events of the Deng period was the massacre of unarmed pro-democracy protesters in **Tiananmen Square** in 1989.

Authoritarian Regime of Jiang Zemin in China

The programs of the Deng regime were, for the most part, continued by **Jiang Zemin**. The government was very concerned with preventing any future episodes like Tiananmen, so the Chinese justice system became even more oppressive. Moreover, Jiang continued the **internal passport system**, which prevented Chinese citizens from moving freely throughout the country. The **Falun Gong**, a group of religious dissidents, was harshly repressed, and **Tibet** was prevented from asserting independence. However, Jiang also promoted the **Special Economic Zone program** and worked to get China admitted to the **World Trade Organization**. He also enabled the campaign that brought the 2008 Summer Olympics to Beijing. Both Macao and Hong Kong rejoined China but were allowed to maintain their local governments, an arrangement known as "one country, two systems." Taiwan declined to enter China this way. In 2002, Jiang Zemin retired at the age of 76.

Structure and Party Makeup of Legislature of Great Britain

Although Great Britain is nominally ruled by a **monarch**, the real power resides with **Parliament**. Great Britain does not have a written constitution; instead, it relies on historical precedent and case law. The country's legislature consists of a **House of Lords** and a **House of Commons**. Membership in the House of Lords is hereditary. This house can create bills, but it does not have very much power. The House of Lords serves as the highest court of appeals in Great Britain. The members of the House of Commons, on the other hand, are elected. This body is run by a **prime minister**, selected by the representatives of the majority party. In recent years, the **New Labour Party** and the **Conservative Party** have dominated British politics, though the **Liberal Democrats** have been gaining prominence. The leadership of the majority party has the responsibility for calling elections, though they must do so within five years of taking office.

Controversial Regime of Conservative Party Margaret Thatcher

When Margaret Thatcher became prime minister of Great Britain in 1979, she vowed to wrest control of the country from the **union leaders** who had gained so much power under Labour Party governments. She also strove to create a more muscular foreign policy, resulting in the **Falklands Crisis** with Argentina in 1982. In 1984 and 1985, Thatcher suppressed striking coal miners, making good on her pledge to marginalize unions. At the same time, she turned several government-owned industries over to private concerns. Some of these businesses included British Steel, Rolls Royce, and British Petroleum. Thatcher discontinued the practice of subsidizing housing, and she sold all houses owned by the state. During her regime, taxes and inflation declined, but unemployment and homelessness grew. She became increasingly controversial, and in 1990, John Major was selected as prime minister by the Conservative Party.

Regime of Conservative Party Prime Minister John Major

John Major was relatively inexperienced when he became prime minister, a situation that was not helped by the almost immediate controversy over Britain's entry into the **European Union**. British people were especially opposed to the idea of adopting the euro and abandoning the pound. Major handled that issue by putting it to a public vote, but his administration continued to be bedeviled by minor scandals and crises like mad cow disease. Though it was perhaps not his fault, Major seems to have presided over the end of a Conservative era in British politics. He resigned in 1995, and the **New Labour Party** took control of Parliament in 1997.

Regime of New Labour Party Prime Minister Tony Blair

In 1997, the New Labour Party took control of Parliament and installed **Tony Blair** as prime minister. Although his party was considered leftist, Blair was more moderate and indeed moved to have **socialism** removed from the New Labour Party's charter. Blair placed a premium on **public opinion** and called for referenda on all sorts of controversial issues, as for instance the relative independence of Northern Ireland, Wales, and Scotland. Blair also queried the British public on EU membership, adoption of the euro, and peace with Northern Ireland. During the Blair administration, Britain adopted a minimum wage law and further diminished the voting rights of the House of Lords. Although the New Labour Party retained control in 2007, Gordon Brown succeeded Blair as prime minister.

Single-Party Authoritarian Regime of the PRI in Mexico

Even though its 1917 constitution made room for multiple political parties in the federal system, Mexican politics was dominated by the **Institutional Revolutionary Party (PRI)** for 70 years. Furthermore, Mexican presidents wielded exceptional power. Although PRI candidates were in control from 1929 to 2000, they changed their positions quite a bit over time. Indeed, the policy swings of the PRI were part of a "**pendulum theory**" designed to maintain control of the government. Each PRI president would handpick his successor, a process known as ***el dedazo***. Of course, the PRI's control was aided by its domination of the news media, which allowed the party to control the information available to voters and repress any attempt at subversion.

Regime of Mexican President Carlos Salinas

Carlos Salinas became president of Mexico under a cloud of suspicion: The computer tallying election results had crashed right after displaying a slim lead for Democratic Party of the Revolution (PRD) candidate Cuauhtémoc Cárdenas. After it had been repaired, the computer showed Salinas in the lead. Despite this dubious beginning, Salinas quickly earned domestic and international support by privatizing highway construction, airlines, mines, banks, and the telephone service, and by joining the United States and Canada in the **North American Free Trade**

Agreement (NAFTA). Unfortunately, any economic progress was undone by a currency crash in 1993, and Salinas's popularity was further diminished by ongoing bloody conflict in Chiapas with a rebel peasant group known as the Zapatistas. Salinas had planned for Luis Donaldo Colosio to succeed him, but Colosio was assassinated in Tijuana in 1994. The blame for this murder and the killing of PRI's secretary general in Mexico City was pinned on Raúl Salinas, the president's brother, who also was caught with a considerable amount of stolen money. Carlos Salinas was so unpopular at the end of his term as president that he had to flee to Ireland.

Regime of Mexican President Ernesto Zedillo

Ernesto Zedillo became known as the "accidental president" of Mexico because he only became the PRI candidate after the murder of Luis Donaldo Colosio. As president, Zedillo borrowed extensively from the United States to shore up the Mexican economy. At the same time, he **modernized PRI** by empowering the *técnicos* (technocrats) and diminishing the power of *los dinos*, the party's old guard. Zedillo also improved the election process by allowing observers, installing computer vote counters, creating voter cards, and establishing an independent election authority known as IFE. Moreover, he broke the tradition of handpicking his successor, instead creating a **primary system** for PRI candidates. Although Zedillo can be praised for these actions, the short-term result was that PRI lost some of its stature in Mexico.

Regime of Mexican President Vicente Fox

With the election of **PAN** party candidate **Vicente Fox** in 2000, Mexico had a president who was not a member of PRI for the first time since 1917. Fox had a background in business, as president of Coca-Cola's Mexican operation, and in government, as governor of the state of Guanajuato. He immediately tried to negotiate a better immigration policy with the United States, but these efforts were unfortunately derailed by the terrorist attacks of September 11, 2001. In the wake of 9/11, the United States was unwilling to cooperate on a deal that would admit more foreigners. At the same time, Fox struggled to reach legislative compromises with the PRI and PRD representatives, and he continued to be weighed down by the ongoing conflict in Chiapas. Though Fox was able to make some positive changes to the Mexican judiciary, his declining popularity was demonstrated by the primary defeat of his handpicked successor, Santiago Creel. In the end, though, Fox was succeeded by Felipe Calderón, another member of the PAN party.

Ibrahim Babangida's Military Regime in Nigeria

Nigeria has endured a series of oppressive military regimes, not the least of which was led by **Ibrahim Babangida**. In 1985, Babangida took control of Nigeria and pledged to restore civilian rule after he had fixed the workings of the government. To do so, however, he claimed that it was necessary to move the capital to an ethnically mixed location, mandate a two-party-only system, take a new census, forbid current and former politicians from seeking office again, and create ethnically mixed states by redrawing boundaries. In a hopeful sign, Babangida called for local elections in 1992. However, when Moshood Abiola appeared to win the election, Babangida invalidated the results, claiming fraud. Violent riots ensued. The popular perception of Babangida was not improved by subsequent revelations that he had amassed an enormous fortune while in office.

Sani Abacha's Military Regime in Nigeria

Babangida's rule was tranquil compared to that of his successor, **Sani Abacha**. Abacha took over control of Nigeria in 1993 and immediately began a campaign of violence against his political adversaries. Abacha's victims included **Moshood Abiola**, who most analysts believe defeated Babangida in the 1992 election, and Abiola's wife. Former leader **Olusegun Obasanjo** was jailed on trumped-up charges, and Nobel Prize-winning author **Wole Soyinka** was forced into exile. Indeed, the Abacha regime drove much of Nigeria's intelligentsia out, which had calamitous economic consequences. A particularly low moment was the execution of ten **Ogonis**, including the writer Ken Saro-Wiwa, who were protesting the destruction of farmland by oil companies, most notably Shell. Abacha's death in 1998 led to the creation of a new constitution known as the **Fourth Republic**. The freed Obasanjo took control of the Nigerian government in 1999 amid great hope, but he was unable to quell the tribal conflict.

Islamic Regime in Present-Day Iran

In the present organization of **Iran**, the most powerful person is the religious leader known as the **faqīh**. The faqīh, at present **Ali Hosseini-Khamenei**, has power over the military, the judiciary, and the media. Iran is a self-styled Islamic Republic with a **unicameral legislature**, whose 209 members serve four-year terms. Iran does not allow political parties, and most political power in Iran is vested in the **Council of Guardians** (which selects the candidates for parliament) and the Supreme Court. From 2005 to 2013, the president of Iran was **Mahmoud Ahmadinejad**. During his term, the nation moved forward on a nuclear program while attempting to diversify its oil-based economy. International observers considered Ahmadinejad's 2009 reelection to be highly dubious. Ahmadinejad was succeeded by **Hassan Rouhani** in 2013, and he remains the current president after being reelected in 2017. Ahmadinejad tried to run for a third term in both 2013 and 2017, but his nomination was rejected by the Council of Guardians both times.

Socialism, Communism, Capitalism, and Mixed Economies

In a socialist system, both the means of production and the land are owned by the state, which means that the wealth generated by economic activity is also distributed by the state. Nevertheless, a **socialist state** may have regular elections and a functional legislative body. The following northern European countries are considered socialist: Romania, Poland, Hungary, Bulgaria, Sweden, Ukraine, Belarus, Russia, and Armenia. The **communist system** is similar insofar as the means of production and the land are owned by the state, but it is typical for political life to be dominated by one party, often in a totalitarian manner. North Korea, Vietnam, Cuba, and China are all communist countries, though China has successfully introduced some elements of capitalism. The **capitalist system** places control of the means of production and the land in the hands of private interests. Finally, in a **mixed economy**, control over the economy is divided between private citizens and the government. In other words, the government controls some functions and leaves others to citizens.

How Fascist Governments Achieved Legitimacy During the 1930s and 1940s

Even the most immoral governments can be **legitimate** as long as they are stable and respected by their own citizens and the governments of other countries. For instance, during the 1930s and 1940s, the **Nazis** in Germany and the **fascists** in Italy achieved legitimacy because they were highly stable and conducted diplomacy with other governments. This legitimacy was achieved despite rampant abuse of human rights by both of these regimes. Similarly, **China** and **Iran** are currently considered legitimate, even though they are notorious violators of human rights and even though Iran is seeking to obtain nuclear weapons against the protests of the rest of the international community.

Communism as the Guiding Principle of the People's Republic of China

In the People's Republic of China, the government is run by a single party, the **Communist Party**. For much of China's history, communist principles like government ownership of the land and the means of production were sacrosanct. However, some of these restrictions have been eased in recent years, and China has become more capitalist. Nevertheless, even though China allows private ownership and supports foreign investors, it remains avowedly communist. For example, the

Chinese government has suppressed all criticism of the communist system, most infamously in the Tiananmen Square massacre of 1989. Suppression of public discourse continues, and in 2000, Google declined to offer some of its services to China amid complaints that the government was using the internet to crack down on dissidents. In 2018, China removed the two-term limit of the presidency that had been established in the 1990s, effectively allowing the current president **Xi Jinping** to remain in office for life. His political philosphies have been amended into the country's constitution known as "Xi Jinping thought."

Socialist States vs. Communist States

In the socialist and communist systems, the government owns the vast majority of the means of production. Indeed, in **communist countries**, the government owns all industry. In China, for instance, the government owns the land, though it is willing to lease out some parcels to private farmers. In a communist state, dissent is not tolerated, and the government strictly controls the information available to citizens. **Socialist states**, on the other hand, do not place all industries under government control. Generally, socialist governments control public services like telephone companies, healthcare providers, and transportation businesses, while leaving other industries to be run by private owners. To fund the essential services under government control, the public is typically charged very high taxes in a socialist system.

Mexico's Decentralized Government

In Mexico, a great deal of political power is vested in the state governments. Each state has a governor, a state legislature, and a state police force. Mexicans vote for local offices and elect people to represent their region in the two legislative bodies of the central Mexican government: the **Senate** and the **Chamber of Deputies**. Although the structure of the Mexican government is decentralized, the domination of the **PRI party** concentrated an inordinate amount of power in the central government for much of the country's history. In 2000, with the victory of Vicente Fox, a member of the heretofore marginal **PAN party**, PRI's rule came to an end.

Centralized Government of Iran

The government of Iran is highly centralized, with most of the power vested in the Islamic leader known as the **faqīh**. The central government creates and passes legislation, and the local governments are tasked with enforcing this legislation. The **Majlis** (legislative body) consists of 290 members who are unaffiliated with any political party, as political parties are illegal in Iran. A set of twelve **mullahs**, appointed by the faqīh and known as the **Council of Guardians**, delimits the authority of the Majlis. For instance, only candidates approved by the Council of Guardians may attempt to enter the Majlis, and the Council of Guardians retains the right to veto any legislation it dislikes.

International Factors Influencing a Country's Public Policy

Public policy can also be influenced by **international factors**. For instance, **economic treaties** will adjust the incentives for various public policy actions. They will also determine the extent to which a country regulates its imports, exports, and tariffs. Many nations have **military treaties** as well. For instance, the United States has declared that it will support Taiwan should the island nation be invaded by China. In some countries, political instability leads to inaction. One example would be Nigeria before 1999; uncertainty about the military government made it difficult for the nation to engage in international trade. Some nations, like Iran, become pariahs internationally and have a hard time cooperating on trade agreements for that reason. Finally, many nations decide public policy issues based on their perceived effects on the value of that nation's own **currency** relative to the currencies of other nations.

Chapter Quiz

Ready to see how well you retained what you just read? Scan the QR code to go directly to the chapter quiz interface for this study guide. If you're using a computer, simply visit the online resources page at **mometrix.com/resources719/gacepolsci** and click the Chapter Quizzes link.

GACE Practice Test

Want to take this practice test in an online interactive format?
Check out the online resources page, which includes interactive practice questions and much more: **mometrix.com/resources719/gacepolsci**

1. Thomas Paine's *Common Sense* influenced which American document that ultimately helped shape the Constitution?

a. The Articles of Confederation
b. The Declaration of Independence
c. The Bill of Rights
d. The Treaty of Greenville

2. One reason the Articles of Confederation created a weak government was because it limited Congress's ability to do what?

a. Declare war
b. Conduct a census
c. Vote
d. Tax

3. The philosophy of the late 17th-18th centuries that influenced the Constitution was from the Age of:

a. Enlightenment
b. Empire
c. Discovery
d. Industry

4. The votes of how many states were needed to ratify the Constitution?

a. Five
b. Ten
c. Nine
d. Seven

5. Virginian ____________ advocated a stronger central government and was influential at the Constitutional Convention.

a. Benjamin Franklin
b. James Madison
c. George Mason
d. Robert Yates

6. Power divided between local and central branches of government is a definition of what term?

a. Bicameralism
b. Checks and balances
c. Legislative oversight
d. Federalism

7. The Senate and the House of Representatives are an example of:

a. Bicameralism
b. Checks and balances
c. Legislative oversight
d. Federalism

8. The civil rights act that outlawed segregation in schools and public places also did which of the following?

a. Gave minorities the right to vote
b. Established women's right to vote
c. Outlawed unequal voter registration
d. Provided protection for children

9. Which court case established the Court's ability to overturn laws that violated the Constitution?

a. *Miranda v. Arizona*
b. *Marbury v. Madison*
c. *United States v. Curtiss-Wright Export Corporation*
d. *Brown v. Board of Education of Topeka*

10. What are the first ten amendments to the Constitution more commonly known as?

a. The Civil Rights Act
b. Common law
c. The Equal Protection clause
d. The Bill of Rights

11. How many Southern states originally ratified the 14th Amendment?

a. Three
b. Five
c. One
d. Ten

12. When the Senate held an impeachment hearing against Andrew Johnson for overstepping his authority, what did they invoke?

a. Checks and balances
b. Bicameralism
c. Legislative oversight
d. Supremacy

13. Which Supreme Court case enforced the civil rights of citizens to not incriminate themselves?

a. Marbury v. Madison
b. Miranda v. Arizona
c. Youngstown Sheet and Tube Company v. Sawyer
d. United States v. Carolene Products Company

14. What judicial system did America borrow from England?

a. Due process
b. Federal law
c. Commerce law
d. Common law

15. The writers of *The Federalist Papers* published under the pen name "Publius." Who were the authors?

a. James Madison, John Jay, and Alexander Hamilton
b. George Washington, Thomas Jefferson, and James Madison
c. Alexander Hamilton, Benjamin Franklin, and Thomas Jefferson
d. Benjamin Franklin, John Jay, and Thomas Jefferson

16. To be President of the United States, one must meet these three requirements:

a. The President must be college educated, at least 30 years old, and a natural citizen.
b. The President must be a natural citizen, have lived in the US for 14 years, and have a college education.
c. The President must be a natural citizen, be at least 35 years old, and have lived in the US for 14 years.
d. The President must be at least 30 years old, be a natural citizen, and have lived in the US for 14 years.

17. The president may serve a maximum of _____ according to the ___ Amendment.

a. Three four-year terms; 23rd
b. Two four-year terms; 22nd
c. One four-year term; 22nd
d. Two four-year terms; 23rd

18. How many Commissioners does the President appoint to the SEC?

a. Five
b. One
c. Two
d. Ten

19. The Office of Management and Budget helps the President prepare the federal budget. What is it a part of?

a. United States Trade Agency
b. Federal Reserve Board
c. Securities and Exchange Commission
d. Executive Office of the President

20. The vice president succeeds the president in case of death, illness or impeachment. What is the order of succession for the next three successors, according to the Presidential Succession Act of 1947?

a. President pro tempore of the Senate, secretary of state, and secretary of defense
b. Speaker of the House, president pro tempore of the Senate, and secretary of state
c. President pro tempore of the Senate, Speaker of the House, and secretary of state
d. Secretary of state, secretary of defense, and Speaker of the House

21. The President has the power to veto legislation. How is this power limited?

I. Congress can override the veto
II. The President cannot line veto
III. The President cannot propose legislation

a. I and III
b. II only
c. I and II
d. I only

22. The president serves as commander-in-chief. What are the president's two limitations in that role?

a. The president cannot declare war or make rules governing the military.
b. The president cannot enforce blockades or declare war.
c. The president cannot enforce quarantines or make rules governing the military.
d. The president cannot enforce blockades or quarantines.

23. What are the official requirements for serving in the House of Representatives?

a. Members of the House must be at least 30 years old, a US citizen for a minimum of nine years, and a resident of the state and district they represent.
b. Members of the House must be at least 25 years old, a natural citizen, and a resident of the state they represent.
c. Members of the House must be at least 30 years old, a natural citizen, and a resident of the state and district they represent.
d. Members of the House must be at least 25 years old, a US citizen for a minimum of seven years, and a resident of the state they represent.

24. What are the official requirements for becoming a senator?

a. A senator must be at least 35 years old, a US citizen for a minimum of seven years, and a resident of the state he represents.
b. A senator must be at least 30 years old, a US citizen for a minimum of nine years, and a resident of the state he represents.
c. A senator must be at least 25 years old, a US citizen for a minimum of nine years, and a resident of the state and district he represents.
d. A senator must be at least 30 years old, a natural citizen, and a resident of the state he represents.

25. Senators were originally chosen by state legislatures. In what year was the constitution amended to allow for them to be elected by popular vote?

a. 1826
b. 1891
c. 1913
d. 1935

26. Who may write a bill?

a. Anyone
b. A member of the House
c. A Senator
d. Any member of Congress

27. Congressional elections are held every ___________ years.

a. four
b. two
c. six
d. three

28. How is a tie broken in the Senate?

a. The president pro tempore casts the deciding vote.
b. The Speaker of the House votes.
c. They vote again.
d. The vice president votes.

29. In order to be accepted, amended, or rejected completely, a newly introduced bill is first given to what type of committee?

a. Full committee
b. Conference committee
c. Subcommittee
d. Senate committee

30. The House Committee on Oversight and Government Reform oversees and reforms government operations. Which Senate committee works with that committee?

a. Senate Committee on Banking, Housing, and Urban Affairs
b. Senate Committee on Homeland Security and Government Affairs
c. Senate Committee on Rules and Administration
d. Senate Appropriations Committee

31. How are members of the Federal Judiciary chosen?

a. They are elected by voters.
b. They are appointed by the president and confirmed by the House of Representatives.
c. They are chosen by a committee.
d. They are appointed by the president and confirmed by the Senate.

32. How long can members of the Federal Judiciary serve?

a. Four years
b. Eight years
c. For life
d. Six years

33. Article III judges who can retire but still try cases on a full-time or part-time basis are called ___________.

a. Recalled judges
b. Senior judges
c. Chief judges
d. Elder judges

34. How many judges are on a panel that decides federal appeals?

a. Five
b. Three
c. Nine
d. Six

35. What petition needs to be filed to request that the Supreme Court hear a case?

a. Writ of certiorari
b. Writ of habeas corpus
c. Writ of mandamus
d. Writ of attachment

36. Most federal judges have served as local judges, lawyers, and law professors. These are ________ qualifications.

a. Formal
b. Required
c. Informal
d. Recommended

37. The Supreme Court has nine members. How is this number determined?

a. It is outlined in the Constitution.
b. Congress determines the number.
c. The President determines the number.
d. The Court decides on the number.

38. Criminal cases are tried under:

I. State law
II. Federal law
III. Civil court

a. I and III
b. II only
c. I only
d. I and II

39. The executive, legislative, and judicial branches of government compose:

a. The federal government
b. The state government
c. Both A and B
d. None of the above

40. Most state governments have a bicameral legislature. Which one of the following states does not?

a. Utah
b. Nebraska
c. Washington
d. Louisiana

41. What does the 10th Amendment establish?

a. Any power not given to the federal government belongs to the states or the people.
b. The president is responsible for executing and enforcing laws created by Congress.
c. Congress has the authority to declare war.
d. The Supreme Court has the authority to interpret the Constitution.

42. Parks and recreation services, police and fire departments, housing services, emergency medical services, municipal courts, transportation services, and public works usually fall under the jurisdiction of which body of government?

a. State government
b. Federal government
c. Federal agencies
d. Local government

43. How is the jurisdiction of federal courts usually decided?

a. By the president
b. By Congress
c. By the voters
d. By the Supreme Court

44. How must inferior courts interpret the law?

a. According to the Supreme Court's interpretation
b. According to the Constitution
c. However they choose
d. According to the political climate

45. How was the vice president chosen before the 12th Amendment was ratified?

a. The president chose the vice president
b. Congress chose the vice president
c. The vice president came in second in the Electoral College
d. There was no vice president

46. What portion of the federal budget is dedicated to transportation, education, national resources, the environment, and international affairs?

a. Mandatory spending
b. Discretionary spending
c. Undistributed offsetting receipts
d. Official budget outlays

47. The primary expense for most state and local governments is:

a. Emergency medical services
b. Transportation services
c. Police and fire departments
d. Education

48. Which court has jurisdiction in bankruptcy cases?

a. State courts
b. Municipal courts
c. Federal courts
d. The Supreme Court

49. Every citizen 18 years of age and older has the constitutional right to vote. What do states govern in the voting process?

a. The registration for and timing of federal elections
b. The administration and timing of federal elections
c. The registration for and administration of federal elections
d. The registration for federal elections only

50. Which statement describes the authority of most local officials?

a. Members of local government are generally elected by the people, but their authority is granted by the state.
b. Members of local government are given their authority directly from the people.
c. Members of local government have constitutionally-granted authority.
d. Members of local government are elected by the people, but the state Supreme Court determines their authority.

51. Which branch of the government employs the Armed Forces?

a. The judicial branch
b. The legislative branch
c. State governments
d. The executive branch

52. The Animal and Plant Health Inspection Service, the Food and Nutrition Service, and the Forest Service are members of which department?

a. The Department of Health and Human Services
b. The Department of Agriculture
c. The Department of the Interior
d. The Department of Transportation

53. A filibuster is used to delay a bill. Where can a filibuster take place?

a. The House of Representatives
b. The Senate
c. Committees
d. The Supreme Court

54. Which organization is maintained by Congress to oversee the effectiveness of government spending?

a. The House Committee on Oversight and Government Reform
b. The Office of Management and Budget
c. Government Accountability Office
d. The Department of the Interior

55. Disagreements between individuals or organizations are tried in:

a. Civil court
b. Criminal court
c. Federal court
d. State court

56. What best describes the way Washington, D.C. is governed?

a. Congress has ultimate authority.
b. Washington, D.C. has a local government similar to that of other cities in the area.
c. There is no local government in place.
d. There is a mayor and city council, but Congress has the authority to overrule their decisions.

57. The Political Affairs Agency is part of which department?

a. The Department of State
b. The Department of Defense
c. The Department of Homeland Security
d. The Department of Security

58. How many Vice Presidents have succeeded to the Presidency mid-term upon the death or resignation of a president?

a. Four
b. Thirteen
c. Nine
d. Five

59. All of the Cabinet members have the title Secretary EXCEPT:

a. The head of the Department of Agriculture
b. The head of the Department of Justice
c. The head of the Department of Commerce
d. The head of the Department of Defense

60. What percentage of votes does the Senate need to pass a bill?

a. Two-thirds majority
b. A simple majority
c. A supermajority
d. Three-quarters majority

61. Which states do NOT generate income by implementing a sales tax?

a. Alaska, Texas, Vermont, and New Hampshire
b. Delaware, Oregon, Texas, Louisiana, and Montana
c. New Hampshire, Oregon, Louisiana, Delaware, and Vermont
d. Alaska, Delaware, Montana, New Hampshire, and Oregon

62. Who negotiates treaties?

a. The President
b. The House of Representatives
c. Ambassadors
d. The Senate

63. There are 435 total members in the House of Representatives. How many are NOT eligible to vote?

a. Four
b. Two
c. Six
d. None of the above

64. Which branch(es) of the federal government issue(s) subpoenas?

I. The executive branch
II. The legislative branch
III. The judicial branch

a. III only
b. I and III
c. II and III
d. II only

65. Who is responsible for ensuring food safety?

I. Federal agencies
II. State agencies
III. Local agencies

a. I only
b. II and III
c. I and II
d. I, II, and III

66. What is the role of the Chief Justice, according to Article I?

a. The Chief Justice heads the Supreme Court
b. The Chief Justice heads trials involving the President
c. The President appoints the Chief Justice
d. The Chief Justice is one of nine Supreme Court judges

67. Which statement is true of an appellate court?

a. The appellate court simply reviews the previous case and does not use new testimony or evidence
b. The appellate court is a new jury trial
c. The appellate court requires new evidence and testimony
d. The appellate court's decision is always final

68. What does the term "en banc" mean?

a. A document requesting an appeal
b. A petition to the Supreme Court
c. A larger group of judges who review an appellate court's decision
d. The legal argument of an appellant

69. Which agency is not part of the Cabinet?

a. US Department of Agriculture
b. Environmental Protection Agency
c. Department of Commerce
d. Department of Energy

70. Which is true of the President's authority?

a. The President has the authority to declare war.
b. The President has the authority to grant pardons and clemencies for federal crimes, except in cases of impeachment.
c. The President can serve three terms.
d. The President has the authority to appoint the Speaker of the House.

71. What would be considered an informal qualification for being elected President?

a. The President must be well-traveled
b. The President must be at least 40 years old
c. The President must have good character
d. The President must be a natural citizen

72. How is a tie in the Electoral College broken to choose the President?

a. Each state's delegation in the House of Representatives gets a vote, and the majority wins.
b. Each state's delegation in the Senate gets a vote, and the majority wins.
c. The former Vice President becomes President.
d. The Speaker of the House casts the deciding vote.

73. Which of the following statements about the House is true?

a. The House tries impeachment cases recommended by the Senate.
b. Each member representing a congressional district is given one vote.
c. The members of the House are elected every three years.
d. The House solely approves any treaty involving foreign trade.

74. Which constitutional requirement is mandatory for a bill to be passed into law?

a. The leader of the majority party decides when to place the bill on the calendar for consideration before Congress
b. The versions of a bill that pass through both houses of Congress and are signed by the President must have the exact same wording
c. The number and kind of amendments introduced in the House are limited
d. A filibuster needs a supermajority vote to be broken

75. How many members of the Electoral College represent Washington, D.C.?

a. One
b. Two
c. Three
d. Five

76. How are federal judges removed from office?

a. They are impeached in the House and convicted in the Senate
b. They are impeached and convicted in the Senate
c. They are convicted in the House and impeached in the Senate
d. They are impeached in the House

77. Cases involving diplomats and ambassadors fall under the jurisdiction of which court?

a. District courts
b. State courts
c. Supreme Court
d. Federal Court of Appeals

78. What does NOT help ensure a two-party system?

a. A winner-take-all system
b. A proportional representative system
c. State and federal laws
d. Political culture

79. What effect do minor political parties have on the elections?

a. They are too small to threaten major parties.
b. They take funding away from major parties.
c. They often work with the major parties.
d. They can potentially take votes away from major parties.

80. Which of the following statements about special interest groups is true?

a. Special interest groups often utilize email and mass media.
b. Business groups generally favor Republican candidates.
c. Special interest groups often file amicus curiae briefs in cases in which they are not directly involved.
d. All of these are true.

81. Delegates awarded to Puerto Rico, Guam, and American Samoa in the Democratic National Convention are:

a. PLEO delegates
b. Base delegates
c. District delegates
d. Bonus delegates

82. What is the main difference between a primary election and a caucus?

a. A primary election is privately run by political parties, and a caucus is held by local governments.
b. Caucuses are always held on the same day, but the dates of state primaries vary.
c. A caucus is privately run by political parties, and a primary is an indirect election run by state and local governments.
d. Primary elections are all held on the same date, but the dates of caucuses vary.

83. What are campaign funds given directly to a candidate called?

a. Lobbying money
b. Hard money
c. Bundling
d. Independent expenditure

84. Presidential candidates are eligible for public funding if they raise $5,000 per state in how many states?

a. Twenty
b. Ten
c. Twenty-five
d. Seventeen

85. What is a committee that raises money for political candidates and is formed by business, labor, or other special interest groups?

a. Party
b. Lobby
c. PLEO
d. PAC

86. What effect do grassroots organizations NOT have on elections?

a. They raise money for campaigns
b. They register voters and recruit volunteers
c. They completely align with party platforms
d. They educate voters and communicate directly to local citizens

87. What are common social demographics for liberals?

a. Single, religious, and educated
b. Single, secular, and educated
c. Married, religious, and educated
d. Married, secular, and gun owners

88. People are typically made aware of political culture, facts, and values through family, friends, society, and:

a. Media
b. Census takers
c. History
d. Gun ownership

89. What does survey sampling help measure?

a. Political values
b. Political socialization
c. Public opinion
d. Private opinion

90. Guaranteed rights enumerated in the Declaration of Independence, possessed by all people, are referred to as:

a. Universal rights
b. Unalienable rights
c. Voting rights
d. Peoples' rights

91. What is the term for the general agreement on fundamental principles of governance and the values supporting them?

a. Rule of law
b. Nationalism
c. Political culture
d. Democratic consensus

92. How do the media and public opinion or polls influence one another?

a. The media does not affect polls or public opinion.
b. The media is unbiased and simply presents candidates.
c. The way the media presents a candidate affects polls, and polls influence media portrayal.
d. The media controls poll results.

93. What do the American labor union movement, the antislavery movement, the women's suffrage movement, and the civil rights movement all have in common?

a. They all used political protest.
b. They all appealed to legal precedent.
c. Thcy all camc from political homogeneity.
d. They were all protected by the commerce clause.

94. What method is NOT used to create a poll?

a. Internet sites
b. Phone interviews
c. Observation
d. Face to face interviews

95. If a party carries a state in a Presidential election, who are named as electors in the Electoral College?

a. Political machines
b. Party activists
c. Executive officials
d. Party workers

96. What type of representation is based on the number of votes each party receives?

a. Coalition
b. Single member districts
c. The Electoral College
d. Proportional representation

97. Which influences are stronger in adult political thinking?

a. Family, media, and class
b. Peers, news, and media
c. Class, peers, and media
d. Family, peers, and news

98. Gun control, strong environmental laws, social programs, and opposition to the death penalty are what kind of issues?

a. Compassion issues
b. Activism
c. Regional issues
d. Religious issues

99. What group petitions the government?

a. Common Cause
b. Party leaders
c. Lobbyists
d. Party activists

100. Political affiliation is an example of what?

a. Personal opinion
b. Schema
c. Public opinion
d. Personal interest

101. How did the attacks of 2001 directly influence American patriotic sentiment?

a. The attacks in 2001 both increased and decreased American patriotic sentiment in different populations.
b. The attacks in 2001 primarily decreased American patriotic sentiment.
c. The attacks in 2001 did not have a large effect on American patriotic sentiment.
d. The attacks in 2001 primarily increased American patriotic sentiment.

102. The constitutional rights of citizens are protected in what?

a. Bicameral legislature
b. Authoritarian regimes
c. Constitutional republics
d. Pure democracies

103. Socialists believe that equality requires:

a. No private property
b. Government influence
c. A free market
d. A mixed system

104. Which supranational institution regulates international trade, human rights, and nation development?

a. The UN
b. The EEOC
c. The UNDP
d. The GOP

105. The media is closely monitored under:

a. The democratic system
b. The Presidential system
c. The authoritarian system
d. The Parliamentary system

106. What was an early difference between Marxism and fascism?

a. Fascism came out of socialism and Marxism from capitalism.
b. Fascists were nationalists and Marxists had an international focus.
c. Fascists wanted to defeat capitalism and Marxists wanted to preserve private property.
d. Marxism originally wanted to preserve class structure and fascism supported capitalism.

107. Public policy is developed at what level?

a. State level
b. Local level
c. Federal level
d. All of the above

108. What are the three stages of the public policy making process?

a. Problems, players, and the policy
b. Religious leaders, cultural institutions, and the private sector
c. Agenda-setting, option-formulation, and implementation
d. Law, decisions, and actions

109. Modern separation of powers preserves which principle?

a. Mixed government
b. Democracy
c. Parliamentary system
d. Presidential system

110. The Head of State and Chief Executive are two separate offices in which system?

a. Presidential system
b. Authoritarian system
c. Parliamentary system
d. Representative democracy

111. What is a similarity between the Presidential system of the US and the Parliamentary system of Great Britain?

a. Both the President and Prime Minister serve as Head of State
b. Both the President and Prime Minister can be removed from office
c. Both the President and Prime Minister are chosen by the legislature
d. Both the President and Prime Minister are elected directly by the people

112. Which system of government formally nationalizes the private sector?

a. Capitalism
b. Corporatism
c. Nationalism
d. Socialism

113. What is the result of a free market combined with government regulation?

a. Mixed economy
b. Corporatism
c. Socialism
d. Nationalism

114. What institution affiliated with the UN is responsible for stabilizing foreign exchange rates?

a. UNDP
b. IMF
c. EEOC
d. PLEO

115. Direct democracy is used more often on which level?

a. National
b. State
c. Local
d. Supranational

116. Special interest groups are considered experts in certain public policy _______.

a. Definitions
b. Processes
c. Implementation
d. Areas

117. Authoritarian regimes often have which type of legislature?

a. Bicameral
b. Unicameral
c. Multi-cameral
d. Representative

118. What does nationalism accomplish?

a. Nationalism legitimizes authority and establishes unity
b. Nationalism creates chaos
c. Nationalism causes division
d. Nationalism causes people to question their leaders

119. What kind of nation is made up of special interest groups that compete to influence public policy?

a. Fascist
b. Communist
c. Pluralist
d. Socialist

120. What do Marxists and capitalists have in common?

a. They both believe in privatizing land ownership
b. They both support free international trade
c. They both support nationalization of the private sector
d. They both support special interest groups

Answer Key and Explanations

1. B: Published in early 1776, *Common Sense* condemned hereditary kingship. The pamphlet was popular in Colonial America, and even George Washington noticed its effect on the general population. Later that same year, Jefferson drafted the Declaration of Independence.

2. D: Congress did not have the authority to levy taxes under the Articles of Confederation. Without the ability to levy taxes, there was no way to finance programs, which weakened the government.

3. A: The Age of Enlightenment was a time of scientific and philosophical achievement. Also called the Age of Reason, it was a time when human thought and reason were prized.

4. C: The Constitution was not ratified immediately. Only five states accepted it in early 1788; Massachusetts, New York, Rhode Island, and Virginia were originally opposed to the Constitution. Rhode Island reluctantly accepted it in 1790.

5. B: James Madison was a close friend of Thomas Jefferson and supported a stronger central government. George Mason and Robert Yates were both against expanding federal authority over the states. Benjamin Franklin was a proponent of a strong federal government, but he was from Massachusetts.

6. D: Federalists who helped frame the Constitution believed the central government needed to be stronger than what was established under the Articles of Confederation. Anti-federalists were against this and feared a strong federal government. A system of checks and balances was established to prevent the central government from taking too much power.

7. A: The Senate and House of Representatives make up a bicameral legislature. The Great Compromise awarded seats in the Senate equally to each state, while the seats in the House of Representatives were based on population.

8. C: The Civil Rights Act of 1964 affected the Jim Crow laws in the Southern states. Many minorities suffered under unfair voting laws and segregation. President Lyndon Johnson signed the Civil Rights Act of 1964 into law after the 1963 assassination of President Kennedy, who championed the reform.

9. B: President John Adams appointed William Marbury as Justice of the Peace, but Secretary of State James Madison never delivered the commission. Marbury claimed that under the Judiciary Act of 1789, the Supreme Court could order his commission be given to him. The Supreme Court denied Marbury's petition citing that the Judiciary Act of 1789 was unconstitutional, although they believed he was entitled to his commission.

10. D: The Bill of Rights was drafted by Congress to limit the authority of the government and protect the rights of individual citizens from abuse by the federal government. It was the first document to detail the rights of private citizens.

11. C: Tennessee was the only Southern state to ratify the 14th Amendment. Although Southern states that ratified this amendment could be readmitted to the Union with more reform, President Andrew Johnson, who was at odds with Congress, advised them against it.

12. A: Checks and balances were established to keep one branch of government from taking too much authority. When Johnson violated the Tenure of Office Act by replacing Secretary of War

Edwin Stanton, Johnson was impeached, but the final vote in the Senate trial came up one vote short of the number needed to convict him.

13. B: The Supreme Court ruled that statements made in interrogation are not admissible unless the defendant is informed of the right to an attorney and waives that right. The case of Miranda v. Arizona was consolidated with Westover v. United States, Vignera v. New York, and California v. Stewart.

14. D: America is a common law country because English common law was adopted in all states except Louisiana. Common law is based on precedent and changes over time. Each state develops its own common laws.

15. A: James Madison, John Jay, and Alexander Hamilton published *The Federalist* in the *Independent Journal* and other publications in New York. It was a response to the Anti-Federalists in New York, who were slow to ratify the Constitution because they feared it gave the central government too much authority.

16. C: The President must be a natural citizen, be at least 35 years old, and have lived in the US for 14 years. There is no education requirement for becoming President. Truman did not have a college education, but most Presidents have had college degrees.

17. B: Most presidents have only served two terms, a precedent established by George Washington. Ulysses S. Grant and Theodore Roosevelt sought third terms; however, only Franklin D. Roosevelt served more than two terms. He served a third term and won a fourth, but died in its first year. The 22nd Amendment was passed by Congress in 1947 and ratified in 1951. It officially limited the president to two terms, and a vice president who serves two years as president only can be elected for one term.

18. A: The Securities Exchange Act of 1934 established the Securities and Exchange Commission, which has five commissioners (one for each division) who serve staggered five-year terms. They are appointed by the President, who also chooses the Chairman of the Commission. No more than three of the commissioners can be in the same party to prevent partisanship.

19. D: The Office of Management and Budget is part of the Executive Office of the President (EOP). The EOP is a group of Presidential advisers and has been in place since Theodore Roosevelt. The President appoints members directly, but some positions like the Director of the Office of Management and Budget need Senate approval.

20. B: The Presidential Succession Act lists the Speaker of the House, president pro tempore of the Senate, and secretary of state next in succession after the vice president. However, anyone who succeeds as president must meet all of the legal qualifications.

21. C: The President has the power to veto legislation directly or use a pocket veto by not signing a bill within ten days after receiving it. Congress adjourns during this time period. A veto can be overridden if two-thirds of the House and the two-thirds of the Senate both agree. The President must veto a complete bill and does not have the authority to veto sections or lines.

22. A: The president of the United States serves as commander-in-chief, but the writers of the Constitution, who feared how authority was used by monarchs, limited the president's power in this role. The president cannot declare war or make rules governing the military, although presidents have traditionally authorized the use of force without war being declared.

23. D: Members of the House must be at least 25 years old, a US citizen for a minimum of seven years, and a resident of the state they represent. Members of the House do not necessarily need to reside in the districts they represent.

24. B: A senator must be at least 30 years old, a US citizen for a minimum of nine years, and a resident of the state he represents. Every state elects two senators, and individual districts are represented in the House of Representatives.

25. C: The 17th Amendment was ratified in 1913. This amendment allowed the citizens to choose their Senators by holding elections and participating in a popular vote.

26. A: Anyone may write a bill, but only a member of Congress can introduce a bill. The President often suggests bills. Bills can change drastically throughout the review process.

27. B: Members of the House are elected for two-year terms. Senators serve six-year terms, but the elections are staggered so roughly one-third of the Senate is elected every two years.

28. D: The vice president also serves as the president of the Senate. If a tie occurs in the Senate, the vice president casts his vote to break the tie.

29. C: A bill is usually first reviewed by the appropriate subcommittee. The subcommittee can accept the bill, amend the bill, or reject the bill. If the subcommittee accepts or amends the bill, they send it to the full committee for review. Expert witnesses and testimony are all part of committee review.

30. B: The Senate Committee on Homeland Security and Government Affairs is a standing committee that oversees and reforms government operations and exercises the congressional power of government oversight.

31. D: According to Article III of the Constitution, Justices of the Supreme Court, judges of the courts of appeals and district courts, and judges of the Court of International Trade are appointed by the president with the confirmation of the Senate. The judicial branch of the government is the only one not elected by the people.

32. C: Article III judges are appointed for life and can retire at 65. They can only be removed from their posts by impeachment in the House and conviction in the Senate. Having judges serve life terms is meant to allow them to serve without being governed by the changing opinions of the public.

33. B: Judges who are eligible to retire but still work are called senior judges. Retired judges who occasionally hear cases are called recalled judges. Both senior and recalled judges handle about 15-20 percent of district and appellate court caseloads.

34. B: The appellant presents arguments in a brief that explains to the three judges on the panel why the trial court was wrong. The respondent explains why the trial court made the right decision. The appeals court usually makes the final decision, unless they send it back to trial.

35. A: A writ of certiorari is filed if a case is lost in appeals or the highest state court. The writ of certiorari is a request for the Supreme Court to hear the case, but it does not guarantee the case will be heard.

36. C: There are no formal qualifications for members of the judicial branch. However, having a background in law is an informal qualification that is considered when appointing Article III judges.

37. B: Congress has the authority to shape the judicial branch. The Supreme Court once operated with only six members. Nine has been the standard number since 1869.

38. D: Criminal cases are tried under both state law and federal law. The nature of the crime determines whether it is tried in state court or federal court.

39. C: State governments follow the example of the federal government and have executive, legislative, and judicial branches of their own, and elected governors who head the executive branch.

40. B: All states have bicameral legislatures, except Nebraska. The bicameral legislatures in states resemble the federal legislature, with an upper house and a lower house.

41. A: The 10th Amendment establishes that any power not given to the federal government in the Constitution belongs to the states or the people. The federal and local governments share many responsibilities.

42. D: Local governments are usually divided into counties and municipalities. Municipalities oversee parks and recreation services, police and fire departments, housing services, emergency medical services, municipal courts, transportation services, and public works.

43. B: Congress normally chooses the jurisdiction of federal courts. The Supreme Court has original jurisdiction in certain cases, which Congress cannot revoke. For example, the Supreme Court has the right to settle a dispute between states.

44. A: The Supreme Court interprets the law and the Constitution. The inferior courts are bound to uphold the law as the Supreme Court interprets and rules on it.

45. C: The 12th Amendment passed in 1804 gave each member of the Electoral College one vote for the president and another for the vice president. Previously, the runner-up in the presidential election became vice president.

46. B: Discretionary spending is dedicated to transportation, education, national resources, the environment, and international affairs. State and local governments use this money to help finance programs. Mandatory spending covers entitlements such as Medicare, Social Security, Federal Retirement, and Medicaid.

47. D: Free public education has been a US tradition since the 18th century. State constitutions govern the educational issues of each state, although federal, state, and local governments all work together on educational issues.

48. C: Bankruptcy cases are the jurisdiction of federal courts. It is not possible to file for bankruptcy in state or municipal courts.

49. C: Nebraska does not require voter registration, but all other states do and have their own process. State and local officials administer federal elections, and though each state has its own method for holding elections, federal elections are always held at the same time.

50. A: The citizens usually elect members of the local government such as mayors and city council. However, the state grants local governments their authority. State and local governments work independently and do not share authority the way the federal and state governments share power.

51. D: The President is the Commander-in-Chief, so the executive branch employs the Armed Forces. When members of the Armed Forces are counted, the executive branch employs over 4 million people.

52. B: The Animal and Plant Health Inspection Service, the Food and Nutrition Service, and the Forest Service are agencies in the Department of Agriculture. The Department of Agriculture ensures food safety, works with farmers, promotes trade, and protects natural resources.

53. B: The House has strict rules that limit debate. A filibuster can only occur in the Senate where senators can speak on topics other than the bill at hand and introduce amendments. A filibuster can be ended by a supermajority vote of 60 senators.

54. C: The Government Accountability Office was originally called the General Accounting Office and was established in 1921 to audit the budget, Congress, and the Director of the Treasury. The Government Accountability Office now oversees the effectiveness of government spending in every branch.

55. A: Arbitration between organizations or individuals takes place in civil court. Civil trials are similar to criminal proceedings and require a jury. Both parties, however, can agree to let a judge decide the case.

56. D: Washington, D.C., as the US capitol, is a federal district. It has a local government in the form of a mayor and city council, but Congress has ultimate authority and can override the decisions made by the local government.

57. A: The Political Affairs Agency is part of the Department of State. The Department of State is an executive agency and the Political Affairs Agency is run by the Under Secretary who supervises the bureaus for Africa, East Asia and the Pacific, Europe and Eurasia, the Near East, South and Central Asia, the Western Hemisphere, International Organizations, and International Narcotics and Law Enforcement.

58. C: Nine Vice Presidents have succeeded to the presidency. Eight of them succeeded to the presidency after a president's death, while the other was in response to a presidential resignation. Four of the nine went on to be elected after finishing the remainder of their predecessors' terms.

59. B: The title Attorney General is given to the head of the Justice Department while every other member of the Executive Cabinet has the title Secretary.

60. B: While the Senate needs a two-thirds or supermajority vote to ratify treaties, only a simple majority is necessary to pass a bill or confirm the appointments of the President.

61. D: State governments are funded by sales taxes, excise taxes, license taxes, income taxes, intangible taxes, property taxes, estate taxes, and inheritance taxes. States enforce some or all of these taxes, but almost all of them utilize a sales tax. Alaska, Delaware, Montana, New Hampshire, and Oregon are the only states that do not have a sales tax.

62. A: The president has the authority to negotiate and sign treaties. A two-thirds vote of the Senate, however, is needed to ratify a treaty for it to be upheld.

63. C: State Representatives all have votes, but the five US territories and the District of Columbia all have Representatives who voice opinions but are not eligible to vote on legislation.

64. C: State and federal courts issue subpoenas for court cases, and Congress has the right to subpoena experts and witnesses for congressional investigations. Failure to respond to a subpoena from either Congress or the judiciary has consequences that could include incarceration.

65. D: Federal, state, and local agencies share the responsibility of ensuring food safety. The federal government provides a small amount of funding to state programs, but state and local programs must find additional funding.

66. B: Officially titled Chief Justice of the United States, Clause 6 in Section 3 of Article I is the only time the position is mentioned: "When the President of the United States is tried, the Chief Justice shall preside."

67. A: Appellate courts simply decide if an administrative agency or trial court made a mistake that influenced the outcome of the trial. The panel of three judges does not use new evidence or testimony.

68. C: The decisions of the appellate court are usually final, but a decision can be reviewed en banc. This happens when a larger group of appeals judges reviews the decision.

69. B: The Environmental Protection Agency is not part of the Cabinet. The Environmental Protection Agency and the CIA are independent federal agencies that are part of the executive branch and are under the President's authority.

70. B: The President has the authority to grant pardons and clemencies for federal crimes, except in cases of impeachment. The House elects the Speaker of the House, the President serves two terms, and Congress declares war.

71. C: Informal qualifications are the public's expectations of Presidential candidates. These can vary, but the President is considered by many to be a moral leader. This means the public expects the President to have a strong character, so a criminal record or lapses in moral judgment can prevent a person from becoming President.

72. A: If there is a tie in thc Elcctoral Collcgc, cach state's delegation in the Ilouse of Representatives gets a vote, and the majority wins. The Senate votes on the Vice President who becomes acting President if the House does not come to a conclusion by Inauguration Day. It is possible for the Senate to tie because the Vice President is not allowed to vote.

73. B: The House has both voting and non-voting members. Each representative of a congressional district is given one vote. The non-voting members are those who represent specific districts, such as Guam, Puerto Rico, and the US Virgin Islands. These regions receive delegates but are not considered congressional districts, and, therefore, their representatives do not receive votes. Choice A is incorrect because the House recommends impeachment cases, and the Senate tries them. Choice C is incorrect because House members are elected for two-year terms. Finally, choice D is incorrect as the Senate is required to approve treaties involving foreign trade.

74. B: The versions of a bill that pass through both houses of Congress and are signed by the President must have the exact same wording. A conference committee brings the versions of the bill into alignment, because the House and Senate versions are rarely identical at first, so a conference committee is often needed to reconcile them into exactly the same wording before final passage in both houses.

75. C: There are 538 electors in the Electoral College. There is one for each member of the congressional delegation. The District of Columbia has three electors in the Electoral College.

76. A: Federal judges are impeached in the House and convicted in the Senate. Judges normally keep their positions for life or until they choose to retire.

77. C: Cases involving diplomats and ambassadors automatically fall under the jurisdiction of the Supreme Court.

78. B: America has a history of a two-party system dating back to the Federalist and Anti-Federalists. Different laws, culture, and a winner-take-all system make it difficult for minor parties to gain ground. America does not have a proportional representative system where the percentage of the population that agrees with a party is directly represented.

79. D: Minor parties often split from major parties and take voters with them. For example, Nader's Green Party was a spoiler in the 2000 election. Gore was down by 500 votes in Florida, and Nader had 100,000 votes in that state. The influence of minor parties on elections often forces the major parties to adjust their ideology.

80. D: All of these are true. Special interest groups utilize e-mail and mass media. They file amicus curiae briefs in cases that do not involve them directly. but the business sector usually favors Republican candidates due to the commonality of pro-business policies supported by Republicans.

81. A: Presidential candidates are nominated at each party's national convention. The Republican and Democratic Conventions have their own processes for selecting delegates. Puerto Rico, Guam, and American Samoa are also awarded PLEO (Party Leaders and Elected Officials) delegates in the Democratic National Convention.

82. C: Political parties organize their caucus as a private event while an official primary is an indirect election administered by state and local governments. Voters may award delegates to candidates for the national conventions, depending on state laws.

83. B: Money given directly to a party candidate is hard money. The Federal Election Commission monitors hard money because of limitations on the amount and the money's source.

84. A: Presidential candidates are eligible for a match from the federal government (with a $250 per contribution limit) if they can privately raise $5,000 per state in twenty states. Candidates who accept public money agree to limit spending. Candidates who do not accept matching funds are free to use the money they raise privately.

85. D: Political Action Committees (PACs) raise money for political candidates and are formed by business, labor, or other special interest groups. They may donate $5,000 per candidate per election, but can contribute larger amounts for party-building activities.

86. C: Grassroots organizations are effective in campaigns. They raise money, register voters, recruit volunteers, educate voters, and communicate directly with people. Grassroots organizations do not necessarily support one of the two party platforms.

87. B: Citizens who consider themselves to be liberal tend to be single, secular, and educated. Conservatives are more likely to be married, religious, and own a firearm. Most Americans do not consider themselves to be extreme liberals or extreme conservatives.

88. A: Political socialization occurs when people are made aware of political culture, facts, and values. Family, friends, society, and the media influence political socialization. Sex, race, age, education, income, and region are also indicators of how a person will vote.

89. C: Survey sampling is used to measure public opinion on different issues such as healthcare reform, the environment, and government spending.

90. B: "...endowed by their Creator with certain unalienable Rights," is excerpted from the Declaration of Independence. These rights are unable to be taken away from individuals, referring to the colonists' rights that Great Britain could not oppress.

91. D: Democratic consensus is the term for the general agreement of the people on fundamental principles of governance and the values supporting them.

92. C: The way the media presents a candidate helps determine polls and public opinion. Candidates who the media presents favorably usually have better numbers in the polls, and candidates who are behind in the polls are often not presented favorably.

93. A: America has a history of organized political protest dating back to the American Revolution. The right to peaceful protest is protected by the First Amendment. The American labor union movement, the antislavery movement, the women's suffrage movement, and the civil rights movement all used political protest to gain support for their causes.

94. C: Surveys used to create polls find people online, conduct phone interviews, and conduct interviews face to face. Mere observation is not used to discover survey information.

95. B: Political activists usually volunteer to work for political parties, and they are chosen as electors in the Electoral College if one party carries a state in a Presidential election.

96. D: Many democratic nations have proportional representation. This type of representation awards representatives based on the number of votes each party receives. Proportional representation encourages multiple parties with focused interests.

97. B: Family, educational systems, peer groups, news, and media all influence political socialization. Adults are more likely to be influenced by their peers, news, and media.

98. A: Compassion issues, such as gun control, strong environmental laws, social programs, and opposition to the death penalty, show a wide gender gap, as women are more likely to support compassion issues.

99. C: Lobbyists for special interest groups petition the government. Special interest groups have been regulated because of their influence and relationships with members of Congress. PACs and special interest groups are both praised and vilified. The group Common Cause wants to end PACs.

100. B: A schema is a belief system that uses personal experiences, socialization, background, and ideological convictions to interpret a subject. A person's political affiliation is an example of a schema.

101. D: Patriotic sentiment is support and devotion to one's nation. The word "nationalism" also refers to the support of one's own nation, often placing the support of one's own nation over worldwide interests. The terrorist attacks of 2001 had an immediate and direct effect of increasing feeling of patriotic sentiment, or nationalism, among US citizens. In the following years, continuous involvement of the US in the war, along with loss of lives, negative economic impact, and changes in national security policies have had a more periodic effect of decreasing patriotic or nationalistic sentiment. These changes in sentiment are more indirect and do not accurately depict the short-term surge of sentiment stemming from the terrorist attacks of 2001.

102. C: The correct answer is C. Constitutional republics provide individual rights in their Constitutions. The people elect representatives, and representatives' policies are moderated by constitutional guidelines.

103. B: Socialism was a movement spurred by the injustices of the Industrial Revolution. True socialists believe in treating all people equally and that the government should be responsible for ensuring that equality. Doing away with private property was the feeling of early communists such as Karl Marx.

104. A: The UN is a supranational institution made up of participating nations that develop international laws. Recent globalization makes supranational institutions such as the UN, EU, and ECOWAS more influential in political policies.

105. C: Authoritarian regimes closely monitor the media. Democratic systems are more open with the media. The independent media of democratic societies is allowed to report on government scandals, corruption, and unpopular policies, which would be suppressed by authoritarian regimes.

106. B: Fascism and Marxism both came out of socialism, and while they had some similarities, they did not support each other. Fascism was focused on specific nations, and Marxism focused on the working class of the world in an attempt to overthrow capitalism. Fascism sought to bring the private sector under government control while preserving private property and class divisions.

107. D: Federal, state, and local governments use laws, regulations, decisions, and actions to address public issues such as healthcare and determine public policy. Members of the private sector, religious leaders, and institutions influence public policy, but the decision lies with the government.

108. C: The process of making public policy has three stages: agenda-setting, option-formulation, and implementation. Agencies and officials meet to discuss the problem at the agenda-setting stage. Option-formulation considers different options for solving the problem and chooses the best option. Implementation is the chosen option being upheld and acted upon by the government.

109. A: The concept of mixed government dates back to antiquity. Plato and Aristotle both advocated a mixture of monarchic, aristocratic, oligarchic, and democratic governments to prevent a single class, state, or person from taking absolute power. The separation of powers in government preserves the principle of mixed government.

110. C: The President is both Head of State and Chief Executive in most countries with a Presidential system. The Parliamentary system divides them into two different positions. The Head of State is often a political figurehead, and the Prime Minister serves as the Chief Executive.

111. B: Both the President and Prime Minister can be removed from office by the legislature. The President can be impeached by Congress, and a majority of the Prime Minister's legislature can cast a "vote of no confidence."

112. D: Socialists feel that capitalism creates inequality. Many believe that nationalization is the answer to ending class distinctions and injustices, while others advocate state control within a free market economy. Corporatism does involve labor, capital, and government working together, but the private sector is not nationalized in corporatism.

113. A: A mixed economy is one that has both elements of free enterprise and the government-run programs often associated with socialism. The United States is an example of a mixed economy since citizens still have a free market, but the government controls sectors such as road repair and construction.

114. B: The International Monetary Fund (IMF) was established in 1944. The IMF works to stabilize foreign trade, reduce trade barriers, and balance trade overall. It has been compared to a credit counselor, but for developing nations. The UNDP provides initiatives and resources to help developing nations.

115. C: Direct democracy is the right of every citizen to attend meetings and vote on issues. A simple majority vote wins in a direct democracy. The logistics for direct democracy, such as holding a meeting for all state citizens, make it difficult for state and national governments to institute. Direct democracy is used on a local level in small New England towns.

116. D: Public policy covers numerous areas, and special interest groups are often associated with areas of public policy. These interest groups publish their research to influence the public policies that are chosen, such as disabilities, health, education, or human rights.

117. B: A bicameral legislature has two legislative houses, such as an upper house and a lower house. This form of mixed government is supposed to ensure greater representation since it takes both houses to pass legislation. Many authoritarian or communist regimes have unicameral legislature, or one legislative house. Unicameral legislatures do not ensure equal representation, but they pass legislation faster than bicameral legislatures.

118. A: Nationalism legitimizes authority and establishes unity. Nationalism or secular nationalism influences world views and seeks to manage chaos. Secular nationalism has influenced the founding and formation of different governments throughout history.

119. C: A pluralist society is made up of many distinct special interest groups that represent different social minorities. These interest groups compete with each other to influence legislation. The power special interest groups exert is constantly shifting.

120. B: Most political theorists support free international trade. For example, many liberals, Marxists, social democrats, and conservatives support the idea of free international trade; however, most communist regimes have strict trade limitations.

How to Overcome Test Anxiety

Just the thought of taking a test is enough to make most people a little nervous. A test is an important event that can have a long-term impact on your future, so it's important to take it seriously and it's natural to feel anxious about performing well. But just because anxiety is normal, that doesn't mean that it's helpful in test taking, or that you should simply accept it as part of your life. Anxiety can have a variety of effects. These effects can be mild, like making you feel slightly nervous, or severe, like blocking your ability to focus or remember even a simple detail.

If you experience test anxiety—whether severe or mild—it's important to know how to beat it. To discover this, first you need to understand what causes test anxiety.

Causes of Test Anxiety

While we often think of anxiety as an uncontrollable emotional state, it can actually be caused by simple, practical things. One of the most common causes of test anxiety is that a person does not feel adequately prepared for their test. This feeling can be the result of many different issues such as poor study habits or lack of organization, but the most common culprit is time management. Starting to study too late, failing to organize your study time to cover all of the material, or being distracted while you study will mean that you're not well prepared for the test. This may lead to cramming the night before, which will cause you to be physically and mentally exhausted for the test. Poor time management also contributes to feelings of stress, fear, and hopelessness as you realize you are not well prepared but don't know what to do about it.

Other times, test anxiety is not related to your preparation for the test but comes from unresolved fear. This may be a past failure on a test, or poor performance on tests in general. It may come from comparing yourself to others who seem to be performing better or from the stress of living up to expectations. Anxiety may be driven by fears of the future—how failure on this test would affect your educational and career goals. These fears are often completely irrational, but they can still negatively impact your test performance.

Elements of Test Anxiety

As mentioned earlier, test anxiety is considered to be an emotional state, but it has physical and mental components as well. Sometimes you may not even realize that you are suffering from test anxiety until you notice the physical symptoms. These can include trembling hands, rapid heartbeat, sweating, nausea, and tense muscles. Extreme anxiety may lead to fainting or vomiting. Obviously, any of these symptoms can have a negative impact on testing. It is important to recognize them as soon as they begin to occur so that you can address the problem before it damages your performance.

The mental components of test anxiety include trouble focusing and inability to remember learned information. During a test, your mind is on high alert, which can help you recall information and stay focused for an extended period of time. However, anxiety interferes with your mind's natural processes, causing you to blank out, even on the questions you know well. The strain of testing during anxiety makes it difficult to stay focused, especially on a test that may take several hours. Extreme anxiety can take a huge mental toll, making it difficult not only to recall test information but even to understand the test questions or pull your thoughts together.

Effects of Test Anxiety

Test anxiety is like a disease—if left untreated, it will get progressively worse. Anxiety leads to poor performance, and this reinforces the feelings of fear and failure, which in turn lead to poor performances on subsequent tests. It can grow from a mild nervousness to a crippling condition. If allowed to progress, test anxiety can have a big impact on your schooling, and consequently on your future.

Test anxiety can spread to other parts of your life. Anxiety on tests can become anxiety in any stressful situation, and blanking on a test can turn into panicking in a job situation. But fortunately, you don't have to let anxiety rule your testing and determine your grades. There are a number of relatively simple steps you can take to move past anxiety and function normally on a test and in the rest of life.

Physical Steps for Beating Test Anxiety

While test anxiety is a serious problem, the good news is that it can be overcome. It doesn't have to control your ability to think and remember information. While it may take time, you can begin taking steps today to beat anxiety.

Just as your first hint that you may be struggling with anxiety comes from the physical symptoms, the first step to treating it is also physical. Rest is crucial for having a clear, strong mind. If you are tired, it is much easier to give in to anxiety. But if you establish good sleep habits, your body and mind will be ready to perform optimally, without the strain of exhaustion. Additionally, sleeping well helps you to retain information better, so you're more likely to recall the answers when you see the test questions.

Getting good sleep means more than going to bed on time. It's important to allow your brain time to relax. Take study breaks from time to time so it doesn't get overworked, and don't study right before bed. Take time to rest your mind before trying to rest your body, or you may find it difficult to fall asleep.

Along with sleep, other aspects of physical health are important in preparing for a test. Good nutrition is vital for good brain function. Sugary foods and drinks may give a burst of energy but this burst is followed by a crash, both physically and emotionally. Instead, fuel your body with protein and vitamin-rich foods.

Also, drink plenty of water. Dehydration can lead to headaches and exhaustion, especially if your brain is already under stress from the rigors of the test. Particularly if your test is a long one, drink water during the breaks. And if possible, take an energy-boosting snack to eat between sections.

Along with sleep and diet, a third important part of physical health is exercise. Maintaining a steady workout schedule is helpful, but even taking 5-minute study breaks to walk can help get your blood pumping faster and clear your head. Exercise also releases endorphins, which contribute to a positive feeling and can help combat test anxiety.

When you nurture your physical health, you are also contributing to your mental health. If your body is healthy, your mind is much more likely to be healthy as well. So take time to rest, nourish your body with healthy food and water, and get moving as much as possible. Taking these physical steps will make you stronger and more able to take the mental steps necessary to overcome test anxiety.

Mental Steps for Beating Test Anxiety

Working on the mental side of test anxiety can be more challenging, but as with the physical side, there are clear steps you can take to overcome it. As mentioned earlier, test anxiety often stems from lack of preparation, so the obvious solution is to prepare for the test. Effective studying may be the most important weapon you have for beating test anxiety, but you can and should employ several other mental tools to combat fear.

First, boost your confidence by reminding yourself of past success—tests or projects that you aced. If you're putting as much effort into preparing for this test as you did for those, there's no reason you should expect to fail here. Work hard to prepare; then trust your preparation.

Second, surround yourself with encouraging people. It can be helpful to find a study group, but be sure that the people you're around will encourage a positive attitude. If you spend time with others who are anxious or cynical, this will only contribute to your own anxiety. Look for others who are motivated to study hard from a desire to succeed, not from a fear of failure.

Third, reward yourself. A test is physically and mentally tiring, even without anxiety, and it can be helpful to have something to look forward to. Plan an activity following the test, regardless of the outcome, such as going to a movie or getting ice cream.

When you are taking the test, if you find yourself beginning to feel anxious, remind yourself that you know the material. Visualize successfully completing the test. Then take a few deep, relaxing breaths and return to it. Work through the questions carefully but with confidence, knowing that you are capable of succeeding.

Developing a healthy mental approach to test taking will also aid in other areas of life. Test anxiety affects more than just the actual test—it can be damaging to your mental health and even contribute to depression. It's important to beat test anxiety before it becomes a problem for more than testing.

Study Strategy

Being prepared for the test is necessary to combat anxiety, but what does being prepared look like? You may study for hours on end and still not feel prepared. What you need is a strategy for test prep. The next few pages outline our recommended steps to help you plan out and conquer the challenge of preparation.

Step 1: Scope Out the Test

Learn everything you can about the format (multiple choice, essay, etc.) and what will be on the test. Gather any study materials, course outlines, or sample exams that may be available. Not only will this help you to prepare, but knowing what to expect can help to alleviate test anxiety.

Step 2: Map Out the Material

Look through the textbook or study guide and make note of how many chapters or sections it has. Then divide these over the time you have. For example, if a book has 15 chapters and you have five days to study, you need to cover three chapters each day. Even better, if you have the time, leave an extra day at the end for overall review after you have gone through the material in depth.

If time is limited, you may need to prioritize the material. Look through it and make note of which sections you think you already have a good grasp on, and which need review. While you are studying, skim quickly through the familiar sections and take more time on the challenging parts.

Write out your plan so you don't get lost as you go. Having a written plan also helps you feel more in control of the study, so anxiety is less likely to arise from feeling overwhelmed at the amount to cover.

Step 3: Gather Your Tools

Decide what study method works best for you. Do you prefer to highlight in the book as you study and then go back over the highlighted portions? Or do you type out notes of the important information? Or is it helpful to make flashcards that you can carry with you? Assemble the pens, index cards, highlighters, post-it notes, and any other materials you may need so you won't be distracted by getting up to find things while you study.

If you're having a hard time retaining the information or organizing your notes, experiment with different methods. For example, try color-coding by subject with colored pens, highlighters, or post-it notes. If you learn better by hearing, try recording yourself reading your notes so you can listen while in the car, working out, or simply sitting at your desk. Ask a friend to quiz you from your flashcards, or try teaching someone the material to solidify it in your mind.

Step 4: Create Your Environment

It's important to avoid distractions while you study. This includes both the obvious distractions like visitors and the subtle distractions like an uncomfortable chair (or a too-comfortable couch that makes you want to fall asleep). Set up the best study environment possible: good lighting and a comfortable work area. If background music helps you focus, you may want to turn it on, but otherwise keep the room quiet. If you are using a computer to take notes, be sure you don't have any other windows open, especially applications like social media, games, or anything else that could distract you. Silence your phone and turn off notifications. Be sure to keep water close by so you stay hydrated while you study (but avoid unhealthy drinks and snacks).

Also, take into account the best time of day to study. Are you freshest first thing in the morning? Try to set aside some time then to work through the material. Is your mind clearer in the afternoon or evening? Schedule your study session then. Another method is to study at the same time of day that you will take the test, so that your brain gets used to working on the material at that time and will be ready to focus at test time.

Step 5: Study!

Once you have done all the study preparation, it's time to settle into the actual studying. Sit down, take a few moments to settle your mind so you can focus, and begin to follow your study plan. Don't give in to distractions or let yourself procrastinate. This is your time to prepare so you'll be ready to fearlessly approach the test. Make the most of the time and stay focused.

Of course, you don't want to burn out. If you study too long you may find that you're not retaining the information very well. Take regular study breaks. For example, taking five minutes out of every hour to walk briskly, breathing deeply and swinging your arms, can help your mind stay fresh.

As you get to the end of each chapter or section, it's a good idea to do a quick review. Remind yourself of what you learned and work on any difficult parts. When you feel that you've mastered the material, move on to the next part. At the end of your study session, briefly skim through your notes again.

But while review is helpful, cramming last minute is NOT. If at all possible, work ahead so that you won't need to fit all your study into the last day. Cramming overloads your brain with more information than it can process and retain, and your tired mind may struggle to recall even previously learned information when it is overwhelmed with last-minute study. Also, the urgent nature of cramming and the stress placed on your brain contribute to anxiety. You'll be more likely to go to the test feeling unprepared and having trouble thinking clearly.

So don't cram, and don't stay up late before the test, even just to review your notes at a leisurely pace. Your brain needs rest more than it needs to go over the information again. In fact, plan to finish your studies by noon or early afternoon the day before the test. Give your brain the rest of the day to relax or focus on other things, and get a good night's sleep. Then you will be fresh for the test and better able to recall what you've studied.

Step 6: Take a Practice Test

Many courses offer sample tests, either online or in the study materials. This is an excellent resource to check whether you have mastered the material, as well as to prepare for the test format and environment.

Check the test format ahead of time: the number of questions, the type (multiple choice, free response, etc.), and the time limit. Then create a plan for working through them. For example, if you have 30 minutes to take a 60-question test, your limit is 30 seconds per question. Spend less time on the questions you know well so that you can take more time on the difficult ones.

If you have time to take several practice tests, take the first one open book, with no time limit. Work through the questions at your own pace and make sure you fully understand them. Gradually work up to taking a test under test conditions: sit at a desk with all study materials put away and set a timer. Pace yourself to make sure you finish the test with time to spare and go back to check your answers if you have time.

After each test, check your answers. On the questions you missed, be sure you understand why you missed them. Did you misread the question (tests can use tricky wording)? Did you forget the information? Or was it something you hadn't learned? Go back and study any shaky areas that the practice tests reveal.

Taking these tests not only helps with your grade, but also aids in combating test anxiety. If you're already used to the test conditions, you're less likely to worry about it, and working through tests until you're scoring well gives you a confidence boost. Go through the practice tests until you feel comfortable, and then you can go into the test knowing that you're ready for it.

Test Tips

On test day, you should be confident, knowing that you've prepared well and are ready to answer the questions. But aside from preparation, there are several test day strategies you can employ to maximize your performance.

First, as stated before, get a good night's sleep the night before the test (and for several nights before that, if possible). Go into the test with a fresh, alert mind rather than staying up late to study.

Try not to change too much about your normal routine on the day of the test. It's important to eat a nutritious breakfast, but if you normally don't eat breakfast at all, consider eating just a protein bar. If you're a coffee drinker, go ahead and have your normal coffee. Just make sure you time it so that the caffeine doesn't wear off right in the middle of your test. Avoid sugary beverages, and drink enough water to stay hydrated but not so much that you need a restroom break 10 minutes into the test. If your test isn't first thing in the morning, consider going for a walk or doing a light workout before the test to get your blood flowing.

Allow yourself enough time to get ready, and leave for the test with plenty of time to spare so you won't have the anxiety of scrambling to arrive in time. Another reason to be early is to select a good seat. It's helpful to sit away from doors and windows, which can be distracting. Find a good seat, get out your supplies, and settle your mind before the test begins.

When the test begins, start by going over the instructions carefully, even if you already know what to expect. Make sure you avoid any careless mistakes by following the directions.

Then begin working through the questions, pacing yourself as you've practiced. If you're not sure on an answer, don't spend too much time on it, and don't let it shake your confidence. Either skip it and come back later, or eliminate as many wrong answers as possible and guess among the remaining ones. Don't dwell on these questions as you continue—put them out of your mind and focus on what lies ahead.

Be sure to read all of the answer choices, even if you're sure the first one is the right answer. Sometimes you'll find a better one if you keep reading. But don't second-guess yourself if you do immediately know the answer. Your gut instinct is usually right. Don't let test anxiety rob you of the information you know.

If you have time at the end of the test (and if the test format allows), go back and review your answers. Be cautious about changing any, since your first instinct tends to be correct, but make sure you didn't misread any of the questions or accidentally mark the wrong answer choice. Look over any you skipped and make an educated guess.

At the end, leave the test feeling confident. You've done your best, so don't waste time worrying about your performance or wishing you could change anything. Instead, celebrate the successful completion of this test. And finally, use this test to learn how to deal with anxiety even better next time.

Review Video: Test Anxiety
Visit mometrix.com/academy and enter code: 100340

Important Qualification

Not all anxiety is created equal. If your test anxiety is causing major issues in your life beyond the classroom or testing center, or if you are experiencing troubling physical symptoms related to your anxiety, it may be a sign of a serious physiological or psychological condition. If this sounds like your situation, we strongly encourage you to seek professional help.

Online Resources

Due to our efforts to try to keep this book to a manageable length, we've created a link that will give you access to all of your online resources:

mometrix.com/resources719/gacepolsci

It's Your Moment, Let's Celebrate It!

Share your story @mometrixtestpreparation